Reflections

(Texas – Colorado – Alaska)

Vonnie Behrend

WESTBOW
PRESS®
A DIVISION OF THOMAS NELSON
& ZONDERVAN

Scripture taken from the Holy Bible, NEW INTERNATIONAL VERSION®. Copyright © 1973, 1978, 1984 by Biblica, Inc. All rights reserved worldwide. Used by permission. NEW INTERNATIONAL VERSION® and NIV® are registered trademarks of Biblica, Inc. Use of either trademark for the offering of goods or services requires the prior written consent of Biblica US, Inc.

WestBow Press books may be ordered through booksellers or by contacting:

WestBow Press
A Division of Thomas Nelson & Zondervan
1663 Liberty Drive
Bloomington, IN 47403
www.westbowpress.com
1 (866) 928-1240

Because of the dynamic nature of the Internet, any web addresses or links contained in this book may have changed since publication and may no longer be valid. The views expressed in this work are solely those of the author and do not necessarily reflect the views of the publisher, and the publisher hereby disclaims any responsibility for them.

Any people depicted in stock imagery provided by Thinkstock are models, and such images are being used for illustrative purposes only. Certain stock imagery © Thinkstock.

ISBN: 978-1-5127-3331-0 (sc)
ISBN: 978-1-5127-3333-4 (hc)
ISBN: 978-1-5127-3332-7 (e)

Library of Congress Control Number: 2016903431

Print information available on the last page.

WestBow Press rev. date: 04/28/2016

Contents

Foreword ix

Reflections in Texas

A Texas Beginnng – Home Sweet Home 3
Enveloped By His Love 5
The House Where God Lived 8
Daddy – All to Myself 10
Nightmare Deliverance 14
Dreams – Yesterday and Today 17
The Benefit of the Doubt 21
The Moth (a lesson learned) 23
Two Heads are Better Than One 26
God Works in Mysterious Ways Indeed 31
Mothers 34
I Am Loved (and so are you) 37

Reflections in Colorado

Greeley or Mom (God's Way or my way) 41
The Tie 44
Sledding and Boulders Don't Mix 46
Marine to the Core 50

Reflections in Alaska

Hidden Beauty in a Frozen and Barren Land 55
The Woman with the Frozen Arm 59
Alaska: Frozen Victory 62
The Tlinget Payback 66
Storms Come to Pass (A thanksgiving tale) 70
Strange Happenings in the Village 75
Bears in the Final Frontier 78
A Dream Come True (at Bonnie Lake) 83
A Memorable Easter 87
Anderson Alaska and the Kids 90

The Dream Song...98
The Unexpected Moose Hunt...100
Hunting vs. Roadkill 107
Finding God in the Pain...112

Reflections of a Widow

The Memorial Service October 11, 2013 119
Alone But Not Alone October 16, 2013............................ 122
Reflections of a Widow November 18, 2013 125
More Reflections of a Widow January 15, 2014.............. 128
Further Reflections of a Widow February 18, 2014.........131
Reflections Once Again April 9, 2014.............................. 134
A Stormy Sea April 15, 2014...137
Reflections of the Past June 23, 2014 139
Reflections on My Birthday July 25, 2014.......................141
A Birthday Blessing July 25, 2014 143
Reflections and Milestones August 4, 2014 145
A Widow's Heart August 14, 2014....................................147
Reflections and Memories September 18, 2014 151
Reflection's Journey November 6, 2014 155
Reflections of Thanksgiving November 28,2014 158
Christmas Hope and Reflections December 23, 2014 160
Reflections of Choices Made 1-20-15...............................163
Reflections of Grief 3-19-15 166
Oscar – A Widow's Friend 168
Alone!! 6-3-15 170
A Widow's Journey 10-6-15...172
Memories of the Man That I Love 12-15-15.....................174

Reflections From God's Heart

A Cut Above...179
Isaiah 40:31 181
A Life Lived Effectively..182
Psalm 27...184
All are Needed...185
Faith..187
Prayer - Called to Righteousness 188

The Promises of God 188
We Were Planned For God's Pleasure 189
Great Things For God (Once in a lifetime?) 190
Isaiah 53 191
Delayed Not Denied 192
Knowing Him: Lord, You Are. 193
Isaiah 58 195
Everyday Blessings 196
Hosea Betroths Gomer 197
Is The Easy Way God's Way? 198
II Chronicles 7:14 200
"Win One For The Gipper" 202
A Springboard For Greatness 203
The River (from a vision given by God in 1999) 205

Reflections in Psalms & Prose

Don't Give Up 209
Live the Dream 210
Welcome to the Family 210
For Such A Time As This 211
Passionate Pursuit 212
Held By Your Love 213
I Have Found a Man 214
Prepare Me 215
Honored to Bow 216
Only Touch Him 217
Favor of God 219
Fully Engaged 220
No Other Way 221
Come, My Child 222
Holy, Just and Pure 222
Consume Me With All Of You 223
I Love You, Lord 224
I Am Loved 225
I Worship You, Almighty God 226
Holy are You Lord 227
In The Glory of Your Presence 228
In Your Embrace 229

Sweet Peace 230
Anointed to Love.. 230
Hush-A-Bye (Tony's song) 231
Sleepy-Bye (Waylon's song).................................231
Little Princess (Lacy's song)................................ 232
Little Green Tractor (Jordan's song).................... 233
At Last He Sleeps (Wyatt's song) 235
Sweet, Precious Child (Tayla's song) 236
Rock-A-Bye (Travis' song) 237
Rain Down From Heaven 238
My Brother's Keeper 239
An Intimate God 240

Foreword

*"Instead of trying to make your life perfect, give yourself the freedom
to make it an adventure, and go ever upward." ~ Drew Houston*

This one phrase, perhaps more than any other, captures the essence
of the lifetime of love shared by my sister, Vonnie, and her mountain
man, Tommy.

I was only nine years old when they got married, and even then
I could sense that theirs was not going to be a dull life. Tommy was
an adventurous outdoorsman; my sister was the city girl who loved
him. And they both had an unyielding passion to follow God's lead,
wherever that would take them.

From the heat of Texas to the Rockies of Colorado to the frozen
tundra of Alaska, they followed HIS lead. They had run-ins with
snakes, scorpions, moose, bears and wolves. They rubbed elbows
with celebrity tourists and hunted game alongside tribal chiefs in
the wild. And somewhere in the process, they lost their hearts to
four little siblings who needed their love.

In the pages that follow, Vonnie paints a vivid picture of a variety
of landscapes. From winters in Alaska lasting longer than most of us
can imagine to the sweltering heat of a south Texas summer… from
the fulfillment of a long unrealized dream of a home brimming
with children to the heartbreaking reality of a spouse gone too soon.
The colors Vonnie uses span the rainbow, conveying light, adding
depth and producing the masterpiece that is a life fully surrendered
to God.

And He is the faithful Presence. He is the miraculous Provider.
He is the One who started them on this journey, warming their
spirits when their world froze over, drying their tears when their
world became too quiet, and holding her close when her world
turned upside down.

So grab a coffee (and a box of Kleenex) and settle in for the adventure of a lifetime... the adventure that is Vonnie's life.

I'm so proud of you, Sis!

Ann Mainse

Hamilton, Ontario, Canada
April 10, 2015

Reflections in Texas

A Texas Beginnng – Home Sweet Home

It all began in Corpus Christi Texas. The tall palm trees waved their happy branches as the sea breeze blew briskly in off the water, only allowing a little relief from the sweltering July heat. A blonde haired, blue eyed baby girl was born on this hot, sultry day, bringing joy beyond imagination to her proud parents. I, Revonne Kay Patterson made my entrance into the world on this summer morning to the sound of sea gulls squawking and tug boats bellowing, as they went on their way through the Gulf of Mexico, right outside the hospital window. The activity and excitement of the morning seemed to give an indication of my life to come. It would be a life of almost constant motion, moving from town to town, state to state and even traveling to other countries.

Texas would always remain home, deep inside my heart. There was a profound love for the diversity I found there, from crashing waves and sandy beaches to the wide open spaces covered with spacious ranches and rich, farm lands. There was flat bottom terrain with tall oaks and pecan trees and then rolling hills covered with scrub brush and tumbleweeds. There were barren deserts and mountains and then tall pine trees in a wooded wonderland.

And despite the horrific heat that would make its appearance each year, the brilliant autumns, mild winters and magnificent springtimes more than made up for the discomfort of summer. I dreamed of and coveted a secret desire to be able to bottle the slightly cold winter weather to then again let it loose to cool the hot humid summer. But it was a silly dream.

However, in the midst of the blistering heat there were other blessings that brought a smile. The sweet smell of roses on a light evening breeze caused one to pause and breathe deeply with a contented sigh. Children playing games as the daylight gave way to dusk, chasing fireflies that shared their unique gift of illumination. Conversations that floated on the air as neighbors sat together visiting on their porches. An unexpected summer shower, which would fill the air with a delightful aroma and bring a refreshing respite from the heat.

The fall introduced a crisp nip to the air with just enough coolness to be pleasant. The pecan trees would drop their treasure of fruit for anyone willing to work a little to harvest and enjoy. The trees would lose their leaves but in South Texas the grass was always green. This was a memory that I would embrace tightly in years to come when I was surrounded by endless white, while living in the majestic mountains of Colorado and barren wilds of Alaska.

In north Texas, the winter brought colder temperatures and sometimes even snow. But in the southern part of the state there was a sigh of relief as the thermometer made a significant drop to comfortable levels. During this time, the migration of many species of birds could be enjoyed daily. There were bright red cardinals, blue jays, robins, hummingbirds and finches just to name a few. I loved sitting out on the patio early in the morning, Bible in hand, as I quietly watched all the birds as they satisfied their hunger at my bird-feeders.

And then there was springtime. The trees took on the most pristine and pure color of green as the new foliage made its appearance. Shortly after, the wild flowers began to carpet the landscape. The pink, yellow, orange and purple buds emerged as if on cue in the fields and the medians of the highways. But my very favorite, other than roses, were the bluebonnets. Oceans of the blue and white blossoms covered the countryside. As a young child, I loved to run through them, sitting down in their midst to breathe in the aromatic fragrance that accompanied their arrival. Ahhh, what a sweet scent. It was a smell that I would never forget, in all of my travels. Bluebonnets portrayed to me the very essence of what made Texas so special. They were strong and sturdy yet beautiful and delicate.

Texas has a heritage rich in history and culture. And as I grew up, I loved hearing the stories about the sturdy pioneers who conquered and worked the land, the emigrants who arrived on ships from other counties to find a new life of independence and faith, the brave men and women who selflessly fought and gave their lives for freedom and all of the diverse people from different cultures that came together to make up this great state. It was in Texas that I experienced and learned about the love of parents, family, friends, teachers and God. It was here that I first hoped and dreamed, learned and achieved, laughed and cried, married and then buried. And despite all of my travels to many unique and beautiful places, Texas remained number one in my heart, for it was home.

Enveloped By His Love

I was born and lived the first few years of my life in the balmy sea breezes of Corpus Christi Texas. Bright sunlight, warm sandy beaches, majestic palm trees and sparkling ocean waves were a part of everyday life. But as a blessed and fortunate child, I was also surrounded by something else. Although I didn't understand the importance or depth of meaning at the time, it molded my young life and paved the way for a wonderful future. Love – I was surrounded by love. Love from my parents, love from friends and family.

But also, there was the love I experienced from the people at church. I got used to being held close and kissed, passed from person to person with smiles. I received hugs and words of affection and affirmation. My blood family wasn't always close by, except for mom and dad, of course. But my church family was always there, smiling and laughing, praying and crying, singing and shouting. I had no siblings in those early years but I had lots of brothers and sisters. Those days and evenings of running, laughing, chasing and playing after services, while the adults stood around talking and visiting, were so carefree and joyful. Sometimes on a warm summer evening when the temperature is just right and the humidity is low, when there's the fragrance of fresh mowed grass or roses in the air, I can still grab ahold of those sweet memories of playing tag or hide and seek with my friends at church. How precious were those moments together.

Then there were the worship services. The singing was so special, such glorious songs of life and praises to God. Sometimes my dad would lead the singing and I would feel so proud. I would sing with even more gusto when daddy would lead. My parents set the example and showed me how to sing with sincere and heartfelt passion. Their love for the Lord was clearly etched on their faces and displayed through every movement and gesture. What splendid times we had in those days. And when the adults were still going strong and I began to grow tired, my mom would lay my head on her lap or put me on a pillow under the pew covered up with her coat. I loved drifting off to sleep to the songs of worship. There were people laughing with pure joy or crying tears of repentance and then relief as burdens were lifted. It was such a wonderful and peaceful sleep I had as a child at our little church.

And then the day came when my church family wanted me to sing a song. I was only three but mom and dad had been encouraging me and singing to me from the womb. I don't remember hearing those wonderful songs while still inside my mama, but surely I must have. I loved music and singing from the beginning. My parents both had beautiful voices and we sang together almost every day. Music was a part of our home, whether humming, singing or playing the radio as the work was done. But the music at church, now that was exceptional, it was so alive and vibrant. People sang from the tips of their toes and the depths of their souls.

So when the time came for me to sing in front of the congregation, I was ready. Even though I was so young, singing was a common everyday occurrence, so it didn't seem scary to me. Of course my family was close by with nods, smiles and words of encouragement. "Jesus loves me, this I know. For the Bible tells me so. Little ones to Him belong. They are weak but He is strong. Yes, Jesus loves me. The Bible tells me so." I sang from the heart and with assurance, for I knew THAT love, it was all around me. My parents, my babysitter Miss Celie and family at church showed it to me daily. I was such a privileged child to be raised within this legacy of love. I knew that Jesus loved me because of the love, safety and security that I found and felt when His presence filled our church and my home.

Every now and then I was asked to sing other songs. My little voice, though not trained, touched peoples' hearts. Before long I found myself standing in front of a TV camera at a local station. They wanted me to sing my song again for more people this time, people that I couldn't see. This was something new and different from singing in my church. There wasn't the familiar crowd of smiling people that I knew loved me. And there was something else that I didn't quite understand. In front of me stood this big camera that I was suppose to look at while I sang. I noticed that I could see myself in the lens, although I didn't know what that was at the time. It was kind of funny being able to see my reflection, like looking in a strange mirror. But with my parents and pastors close by, the camera didn't appear too scary, it just looked really big. So wearing my new blue velvet dress and with my blonde curls bouncing up and down, I sang about Jesus' love once again. I could feel Him close by, no fear, just an atmosphere of peace and love. The song was sung before I knew it and then once again I was being held, tickled, hugged and kissed.

As I look back now and remember those happy childhood days, I realize that I was so blessed to be surrounded by such an atmosphere of love. Fortunately, it didn't end there. I have found all through the many years of my life, whether in Texas, Colorado or Alaska that with Jesus, my extended family and amazing friends all around me, I am continually ENVELOPED BY HIS LOVE.

The House Where God Lived

As an eight year old child and having been raised to know the Lord, I was aware of His presence in my life. I knew the love of family and friends. I knew the Bible stories and went to bed each night with a prayer on my lips. However, knowing the Lord and understanding all about Him are two very different things. I knew that He was loving, kind and compassionate but I also knew that He was powerful, awesome and to be respected. After all, He is The King and Creator of everything. So in my young mind, He must dwell in an unusual yet awe-inspiring house.

Such a house stood tall and proud along the street that led to my elementary school in Dallas Texas. Most mornings and afternoons I would walk by this old house and look at it curiously. On many of those days, one of my friends, either Nadine or Darrell, would be by my side. As we walked, we would talk, wonder and speculate about this lovely old home. It stood three stories tall, a gingerbread house with dormers and lattice work. There were stained glass windows on either side of the front door and above the front windows. The neglected flower beds held a wide variety of wild flowers in the late spring and early fall. But in April, a beautiful array of bluebonnets covered most of the front yard. It was an awesome and heavenly sight. To my innocent thinking, the house was grand and beautiful and yet it appeared empty.

One day, on our way to school, Nadine and I came to a decision. After school that day, we would stop and explore the charming, old house. While at school, we expectantly and excitedly waited for the final bell to ring. When it did, we walked, skipped and ran all the way to 'God's special house'.

We started our inspection by walking all the way around it. We checked the front and back doors but both were locked. We were able to see in a few windows on both porches but the rooms looked dark. Checking carefully, we were able to see that the house was indeed empty. The windows on the sides of the house were too high for our small frames, so we gave each other a boost to see as much as possible. During one of these peeks, we discovered that one window was cracked open a tiny bit. We were overjoyed, for now we could truly explore. As we pushed and shoved, we were able to get the window open wide enough for us to wiggle inside. Climbing into that old house and standing in that musty bedroom was so thrilling, that we could barely breathe. "Surely this was a house where God lived" we whispered to each other. The rooms seemed so massive and the staircase in the hall stood tall and impressive. We were certain that we stood on holy ground. As we explored, we didn't run and yell but walked reverently, talking in hushed tones. We were in awe. We climbed the rickety old stairs to the second floor, looking into closets and out the windows of each room. We looked up the staircase to the third floor attic but didn't dare to go that far. We loved peering out the stained glass windows and tracing the beautiful patterns their reflection made on the floors and walls, as the waning sunlight shone through. There was no furniture, just an old brass candlestick holder and a few hangers. And yet to our young minds, we were certain that God must visit this place.

Not soon enough, we became aware that the time had hurried by and that our families would wonder where we were. So we whispered a respectful goodbye to 'God's special house' and climbed back out the window. When outside, we realized that we had taken way too long on our quest, so we ran the rest of the way home. My friend Darrell met us at the top of the hill, to warn us of our parents worry. We had been in that old house for almost two hours. The police had been called and the search had commenced. When we arrived home, we were greeted with relieved hugs and kisses followed by the belt of correction. Stern warnings were issued about danger and safety, fears and worries. Even in the midst of our repentance and promises to never repeat such an act, there was the lingering feeling of wonder that we had felt on that day and in that special place.

Now as an adult, when I think back, I can still grab hold of that feeling of reverence and awe that we experienced. I know that the old house was not necessarily a place where God lived and yet, IT WAS, because God lived in Nadine and me. So on that day, He did dwell or live in that house. That awesome, tangible presence that we felt was real. Two innocent, naïve little girls were held in the palm of God's hand as they explored a rickety old house with many unseen dangers. As we walked through those rooms and climbed the old rotting stairs, He was right there with us, protecting and holding us. Thankfully, that day, that grand old house was "The house where God lived".

Daddy – All to Myself

Ever since my parents divorced when I was nine, I had spent a month almost every summer with my dad, second mom and siblings. These times together, always produced happy memories of travel, new adventures, amusement parks, games and lots of laughter. We always had a happy, wonderful time together. But the second summer, after my parent's divorce and before my siblings came on the scene, proved to be one of the most memorable and special times for me. My dad was stationed at Fort Sam Houston in San Antonio, so I went to spend that month with my family on the base. My little sister was due to be born in September, but my second mom was having a very difficult time. She had to remain on bed rest and even in the hospital for the last two months of her pregnancy.

When I arrived for my vacation, I found out that, this time, it would be just me and dad. And even though my new mom was always very loving and showed her acceptance of me, I was thrilled to have daddy all to myself. He explained that I would be the lady of the house and that I would need to fill in for my new mom. I would have the responsibility of taking care of him while she was in the hospital. I was so excited to be able to cook for my daddy, to clean the house, to do his laundry and make sure his needs were met. "My daddy needs me" I thought. It was like a healing balm was being poured upon my wounded heart, since we had been apart for quite a while. And even though I was only ten, I started making plans for the lunches and dinners that I would prepare for him. Dad also had his own ideas for what we would do together after he got off work in the evenings. Bubbling with excitement, I began telling him all about my thoughts for our meals. He didn't discourage me but did let me know that the evening meals would mostly be his responsibility but that I could definitely assist him or be his escort out to dinner. Wow, I would be my dad's dinner date, going to a real restaurant, just the two of us!

We sat down and began to map out our month together. During the week, dad would go to work then come home at noon. I was happily in charge of preparing lunch each day. I already knew what his preferred foods were and we stocked up on all of the ingredients during one of our shopping trips to the commissary. Among his favorites was a special beef sandwich. It was garnished with mayo, lettuce and tomato and the bread had to be toasted just right. He was also quite fond of soup, pot pies, grilled cheese sandwiches and BLT's. I felt so important to be given this special job to do for my dad. Every day, he would come home to a hot lunch served on a special plate with a placemat and napkin. I would decorate the plate with a side of pickle, a slice of tomato or some olives on a toothpick to add color. When he saw my efforts, his bright smile, that went all the way up to his eyes, melted my heart. I knew that he was pleased and proud of me. He would tell me all about his morning activities and we would talk over my plans for the afternoon. After lunch, we cleaned up the kitchen. What a happy time we had just eating and talking at our small kitchen table.

Then in the afternoon, he would go back to work. Sometimes, I would go for a ride on the bike he had rented for me to use while I was there. When I did this, he always required that I come by his office on the base, which was only about two miles from the house. I loved going by his office because I was so proud of him and knew that he held a position of importance. In those days, he was a 1st Lieutenant in the U.S. Army. His office staff always greeted me warmly and daddy always had a big smile for me. Sometimes he would give me money to go to the base theatre for a movie or I would ride to the local pool to swim for a few hours. And then on the way home, I would go back by his office to check in with him so he knew that I was safe. Sometimes I would stay at the house and watch TV but usually I was out and about on my bicycle. Occasionally, he was able to leave work a little early and we would go home to get his bike so we could ride around the base together.

On one of my bike outings to the swimming pool, I ran into a very unique problem. As usual, I stopped by the office to check in and then went to the pool. When I arrived at the outdoor pool, everything was very neat and fresh looking. I guess they had taken extra effort to clean the facility. I parked my bike, put my things away in the locker with my trusty combination lock and went for my swim. I was quite a good swimmer since taking lessons at the YMCA. My mom had made sure that I learned since I almost drowned twice when I was younger. I could swim like a fish now and had earned several badges from the American Red Cross. I also enjoyed diving off the high dive. My afternoon passed by swiftly as usual. And not noticing anything out of the ordinary, I dried off and gathered my things. The bike ride helped to finish drying my damp clothes and hair. However, when I walked into dad's office this time, people looked at me rather strangely. They were still smiling but with a quizzical look on their faces. I looked down at myself, wondering if I had forgotten to button or zip something. When I walked into dad's office, He also looked a little perplexed . He got up from behind his desk and walked over to me. Looking at me curiously, he brushed my hair back with his hand. "Is something wrong, daddy?" I asked. He kind of laughed and steered me over to a mirror on the wall. I turned and looked and couldn't believe my eyes. My platinum blonde hair was now a pale, but distinct shade of green. I hadn't looked in a mirror at the pool, so I didn't know. What could have happened? My eyes began to fill with tears, but dad quickly assured me that somehow we would get the color out of my hair. The mystery was, "How did it get there?" Daddy made a few phone calls and found out that the swimming pool had been thoroughly cleaned and fresh chemicals had been put in over the weekend. No one really knew why my hair had turned green but as it turned out, I was not the only one. Sometime later, we learned that an imbalance of chemicals in a pool can cause this condition for blondes. On that day, my dad took off work early, taking his teary-eyed daughter home to attack the problem at hand. And the solution to that problem was about six washings with a special shampoo. Sure enough after a few hours of washing and rinsing, the green color was gone and I was a blonde again. Thank the Lord for PRELL shampoo.

Most days, when dad would get off work in the evening, we would go by the hospital to visit mom, although dad was only able to sneak me in to see her once. In those days, children under the age of twelve were not allowed in the hospital rooms. Then after our visit, we would go home and fix dinner and play board games all evening. Sometimes we would get a hamburger and then go play putt putt golf. But there were a few times when we went home and dressed up and went out to a nice restaurant. These were very special and made me feel so grown up. Daddy would open my door and pull out my chair for me to sit down. We held handsas we prayed over our food, and then he would look into my eyes, kiss my hand and say 'I love you, sweetie'. When he introduced me to friends and co-workers, I felt so important and adored. I was the center of his world and attention. Afterward, he would put me to bed with lots of tickles and giggles or he would turn on the stereo and we would have a bedtime dance to Floyd Kramer's "Last Date". Then he would tuck me in, say prayers and I would drift off into a very happy sleep.

That summer alone with daddy has stayed with me all these years and has been one of my happiest memories. The remembrance of the love that I experienced helped to carry me through all of the lonely months to follow, when we would be apart because of the divorce and two year-long deployments to Vietnam.

It's no wonder that my view of the Heavenly Father is so positive. I know what it means to be loved and treasured by an earthly father, even though he wasn't perfect. How much more must my Heavenly Father, who is perfect, love me. The thought is astounding and beyond my limited understanding. Some people don't have that assurance of the Father's love because they were deprived of their dad's love when they were young. Maybe he was physically or verbally abusive. Perhaps he was just too busy making a living to give the needed attention. Whatever the reason, I can assure you that God, the Father, adores you and wants you to feel loved and cherished. Believe it to be true and it will make all the difference in the world to how you face life. Knowing that you are accepted and adored09 can help bring you through anything.

I had never shared these thoughts with my dad until the last year of his life. At the age of 67, his cancer had returned after being in remission for eighteen months. The doctors gave him six months to live and because of that we were able to sit down and share some things from our hearts. He was so surprised when I told him about the depth of meaning of that summer. To him, it had also been a special time together but he didn't realize the exceptional significance it had held for me.

What a happy memory – Daddy, all to myself.

Nightmare Deliverance

When I was a teenager in high school, I experienced a recurring nightmare for several weeks. Once or twice a week it would come and I dreaded it because it was very frightening. Mother and I lived in an apartment complex called Randolph Manor in Dallas. It was quite nice back in those days with about 200 units. The units were interconnected in several grids of rectangles. In the center of the complex was a playground and a pool area. It was one of my favorite places to hang out during those 100 degree summer days when you could fry an egg on the hood of your car. Our apartment was only about 200 feet from the pool. I loved to swim and after my initial, beginning of the summer sunburn, I usually acquired a nice tan. We lived there for about five years and were settled and happy with many friends and neighbors. The reason for the nightmare was never really apparent to me since it was a pleasant place to live and make memories. I never knew when the dream would occur, since there was nothing I could put my finger on, that triggered it.

The nightmare would begin with me outside of our apartment after dark, calmly walking around, enjoying the cooler evening breezes. At one point I would get the feeling that someone was watching me and would become apprehensive. I began walking more swiftly with the purpose of getting home to safety. And then I would start seeing shadows darting in and out around me and could hear a man's low, malicious laugh. I knew he was coming after me so I began to run, trying to escape him. Every now and then I would catch a glimpse of him chasing me as I rounded a corner. But no matter where I ran, I couldn't seem to find our apartment and with each turn he was gaining on me. He was dressed all in black, with a black cape, mask and hat and I instinctively knew that he was very evil and wanted to harm me. At some point in the chase, every time I had this nightmare, he would catch up with me. As soon as he grabbed my arm, I would freeze. I was unable to move, fight or even scream. I was terrified as he came close to me, leering at me with glowing, ruthless eyes. Even lying in my bed, I would partially wake up but would be unable to move. As I struggled to do SOMETHING, I was finally able to wiggle my little finger, then my hand, then my arm and eventually I was able to sit up on the side of my bed, sweating and trembling with fear. At first, I shook off the terror and lay back down, relieved that it was only a dream. But I soon learned that if I went right back to sleep, the nightmare would begin all over again and run the full course of horror. It always ended the same, with him catching me and me freezing up in the dream and in my bed. Week after week, I battled this cruel fantasy, not understanding why I was being plagued with it. I discovered that if I would get out of bed and walk around or get a drink of water, I wouldn't have it again on the same night. But the dream continued none the less. Then finally, after several weeks of this torture, I remembered who I was in God and I took a firm stand on His Word and in His Authority.

During this time in my life and thanks to the sacrifice of my hard-working, single mom, I was heavily involved in our youth group and choir at church. Each year, there would be a contest where high school students could be crowned queen and king or named as part of the royal court at a special banquet. Everyone who faithfully participated, was awarded some really nice and even expensive prizes. Each student could earn points by inviting and bringing people to church, reading through the entire Bible, taking a detailed quiz, memorizing hundreds of scriptures, being faithful in attendance and serving in the church, etc. This event went on for about three months in the spring. I participated in the competition for three years, winning it in my senior year. It was quite intense and actually proved to be an invaluable tool and resource for helping me to mature in the Lord. It was not a frivolous thing but required extreme dedication and a LOT of hard work.

Some of the scriptures that I had memorized were about God not giving us a spirit of fear, about resisting the devil and him fleeing, about the Angel of the Lord encamping about us and about taking authority over the enemy and vain imaginations through Christ. After several weeks of struggling with the nightmare, these scriptures began coming to my mind. So when I woke up and was finally able to move around, I began taking authority in Jesus name, over this spirit of terror and the one who sought to torment me. It took three nights of standing firm on the Word of God in Jesus name before my deliverance from this horrible dream came. But finally it did come and I was never plagued with that nightmare again.

Now throughout my life, the enemy has continued to try to bring about fear over various situations and even through other dreams, but I know how to fight him now. God's Word is powerful and is intended for us to use as a weapon against the father of lies. I am so thankful that the adults in my church, Bethel Temple, decided to work so hard and give so much of their time and money to provide that incentive for their youth to learn scripture. I didn't realize the value of this knowledge when I was in the midst of the process. But later as I walked around my bedroom quoting those wonderful Words of Life and finding that deliverance, I began to understand the precious treasure that they had afforded me.

And now as an adult, having gone through many trials and testing, I know the importance and necessity of having God's Word in my mind and close to my heart. If you haven't found this treasure, it's right there beside you. Start memorizing today. Write the Word on a card and place it on the fridge or on your bathroom mirror. It won't take long to have it firmly established. Put it there now before a desperate need arises. You will be so glad that you did. And if you are tormented by the enemy with nightmares, fears or vain imaginations, God's Word and the name of Jesus will pull you through. He is there for you and is expectantly waiting for you to call on Him, the Deliverer and Lover of Your soul.

Dreams – Yesterday and Today

I am a dreamer. I guess that is the way God created me. From a child, I can remember dreaming quite often. As with most people, many of my dreams were just silly or even strange, caused by who knows what, maybe the pizza I had the night before. But some of my dreams had meaning. A few of them were a direct message from the Lord and I knew it.

ROLLERCOASTER TO HEAVEN - One of the silly dreams I still remember to this day was my dream of going to heaven on a roller coaster. This was in my younger years when amusement parks and enjoying these types of rides was a yearly event. In my dream, I was alone in my own particular coaster car and I was the only one on the track. I remember starting out on level ground and then climbing higher and higher into the clouds. But before long, I was whizzing down at an exhilarating speed, which always thrilled me. Throughout the years, I thoroughly enjoyed my roller coaster rides, going on all kinds, even ones that did the loops and the cork-screw. But in the dream it was just the excitement of up and down through the clouds. At one point the ride dipped way down and instead of clouds I could see fire and smoke. A creature, that I thought might be the devil stood far off to the side laughing as though he thought he could get me. But then I soared up even higher and higher and higher. I knew at this point that I was getting a glimpse of heaven with beautiful clouds, brilliant colors, angels and music filling the atmosphere. It was then that I awoke knowing that the Lord had me in the palm of His hand. Now, whether this dream was pizza induced or not, I don't know. But I do know that I came away from it with a smile and an assurance that all was right with me and the Lord.

RAPTURE - On a different occasion, I dreamed that I was caught up in The Rapture of the church. I remember feeling the weightlessness as my feet left the ground. The sky had a rich golden hue to it and was full of big white, fluffy clouds. As I looked up, I could see a brilliant light higher up in the sky. I remember straining to see the Lord Jesus, because I was sure, somehow, that He was within that light. I never actually saw Him in this dream. As I rose through the air, I was filled with an incredible sense of joy never experienced before. I could see other people rising through the air also, but I didn't recognize anyone. The main feeling that stayed with me for weeks and months afterward was the exhilarating sense of flight and weightlessness. But even more than that was the excitement of knowing it was the rapture and that I would see Jesus.

UNFORGIVENESS – Some dreams you just know are from the Lord and this next one fits securely into that category. Many years ago, after we had returned from Alaska, just before the kids came back into our lives again, I was jolted into reality by a dream from the Lord.

In my dream, Tom and I were doing well and life was progressing on an even keel. I thought that everything was in good order. Unexpectedly, in my dream, I died and stepped into eternity. As soon as I passed away, I knew immediately that something was wrong, because a horrible weight of darkness rested on me. I didn't feel the bliss of knowing that I would soon see Jesus and all my loved ones who had gone on before me. All I felt was a sense of emptiness, aloneness and dread. Where was the joy and laughter, the glorious light and vivid colors, the beautiful music and vibrant harmonies that I had experienced several years earlier in a dream? But mostly, where was Jesus? My heart sank in a hopeless heap of fear and horror as I realized that I had held on to unforgiveness for people who had crushed and wounded me. And somehow in that moment I knew that because of this, I was forever separated from my Lord. I began to weep uncontrollably, begging the Lord to cleanse me and to give me another chance to make things right in my own heart and with the people involved. And then I woke up! What an overwhelming relief, it was just a horrible dream! I had another chance, all was NOT lost. I could forgive and be reconciled with the ones that had hurt me so deeply. At that very moment, I prayed and spoke words of forgiveness over those people and then ask the Lord to forgive me. To be honest, I didn't really FEEL the forgiveness take root in my heart for several weeks. But I continued to verbalize it to the Lord every day. And when I saw them or heard from them, I didn't avoid talking to them. The hurt and anger began to dissipate until I was finally able to truly forgive from the depths of my heart. This sincere forgiveness did take some time and purposeful determination. After that, I tried to do a heart check every now and then to make sure that I wasn't harboring any offenses, grudges or wounds. I never again want to feel that sense of utter aloneness and hopeless dread that I experienced in that dream. But I am thankful that the Lord allowed me to have it, as a warning and a wakeup call.

FAMILY - The Lord has also honored me with dreams or visions of some of my family that have gone to heaven. My cousin Jimmy was such a special person with a beautiful contra tenor voice. One evening, on my way home to Anderson from a shopping day in Fairbanks Alaska, I had a waking dream. It was summertime and the sky was a beautiful golden color as the evening sun began to go down over the horizon. In that moment I saw Jimmy singing with a vast and brilliantly robed choir. He was beaming with that special smile of his and singing from the depths of his heart. It gave me the assurance that all was well with him.

Another time, after my mama and second mom went to heaven, I saw them and my daddy together in heaven. In the dream, I was walking down a brownish, golden path on a beautiful, green grass-carpeted hill. At the base of the hill there was a long, meandering, crystal stream sparkling in the distance. There were multi-colored flowers growing everywhere on the grass and on bushes. Before the stream, there were several people milling around and sitting on ornate white benches. There were tall, majestic trees spreading blossoming branches over them as they visited with one another. As I drew closer, I could see that three of the people were my parents. They were all dressed in different shades of white, Victorian-type clothing and they were so beautiful. They were talking and laughing in a carefree, joyful manner. And as I watched, they turned, smiled and waved to me. Then I woke up with a satisfied sigh and a smile on my lips. What a lovely dream.

My most recent dream was of my husband Tom. About a month after he died, I had a brief encounter with him in a dream. Suddenly he was there in front of me, smiling at me. I was overjoyed to see him. He held out his arms and as I ran to him, he embraced me and began to whisper something in my ear. In my excitement to be with him, I didn't hear what he said and so I had to ask him to repeat it.

"Don't quit singing, Sugar. Keep on doing what you love and were created for." Then he hugged me again, smiled and was gone. I believe that God allowed that dream as an encouragement to me. There have been so many times since his death that I have wondered what I was supposed to do now. Our lives and future had always been tied together and going forward alone has been very difficult and challenging. About two months after my special dream of Tom, I heard a song on the radio that spoke to me deeply. The chorus described my dream so beautifully that I had to purchase the sound track and have been singing it at different events and services where I have been asked to minister. The song is called "On the Other Side" and the chorus goes like this: "Well I've never been to heaven, didn't know what it was like, but God let me have a glimpse in my dream last night. And I could see you smiling, you were looking right at me, and I knew that you were happy, on your face I saw sweet peace. And I knew everything was gonna be alright, on the other side." Now you understand why I was so drawn to the song. Again the Lord sent comfort my way, this time through a song.

The Lord is so good and faithful to keep me in every situation. He continues to encourage and give me words of wisdom and comfort in various ways, from His precious Word, through friends and in SPECIAL DREAMS.

The Benefit of the Doubt

It has been a long standing belief of mine to give people the benefit of the doubt. In other words, I have tried to live in a way where I'm not suspicious of their motives. If something is said that could be taken in a good way or a bad way, I've always leaned toward believing that they meant that particular comment for the good. I fail to see the value of believing the worst about people, rather than the best. Let's face it, sometimes our words and actions just don't come across as we intend. I know that I hope others will believe the best of me, so I try to afford them the same courtesy. The catalyst that triggered this life-long policy of looking for the positive in others came about when I was seventeen and quite naïve.

During this time in my life, I had the privilege of being asked to be part of a Youth Choir that would be traveling all over Europe for seventeen days. We would visit and minister in nine different countries. One of the cities where we toured and sang was Paris, France. What an exciting time we had there, visiting the Eiffel Tower, Notre Dame, museums and cathedrals. We were scheduled to sing at a rather large and impressive cathedral on one of the major thoroughfares in Paris. Advertisements had gone out and posters had been distributed. We were hoping for a good crowd.

The night before the performance, we went to the Church to rehearse and prepare. The ornate chapel was equipped with a massive pipe organ which our pianist was able to learn how to manipulate and play. We also had a drummer, bass player and guitarist. Some of our songs would be played by the pianist and by the other band members. Other songs would be acapella. Everyone was in a good mood with lots of laughter and fun. The rehearsal went fairly smoothly until we practiced the song 'Oh Happy Day'. This song was very upbeat and was normally played on a piano or keyboard, but for this concert it would be played on the pipe organ. After running through the song a couple of times, I leaned over to a friend and said, "I like this song better on the piano". The mother of the pianist, who was one of our sponsors, overheard my comment and became very angry with me. In front of the entire choir, she berated and humiliated me for my "offensive and judgmental comment about her son's abilities". I apologized to her, trying to explain that I meant no offense or criticism of him. In fact, I was in awe of his talent and thought very highly of him. But nothing I said could sway her or make her realize that the comment was innocent and just an observation. She went to her husband, who was the leader of the group, telling him her view of everything. I was taken aside and scolded for my insensitivity and cruel comment. Again, I tried to explain but she was very adamant with her accusations so no one really listened to me. Her anger was so intense, that at one point, I wondered if somehow they would find a way to send me home early. I felt utterly alone, away from my family in a foreign country, with just a few people that I knew well. The practice resumed, but without me, because I was so deeply hurt and wounded. A dark cloud had settled upon me and I felt a great sense of rejection and alienation. Later, some of the other choir members and even some sponsors, who actually heard the comment, came to me with words of comfort and to show their support. For a few days, I was shunned by some of the group until word spread about what had actually happened. Most of the group came to understand and accepted me back into their circle, but that mother never did.

It took me many years to recover from the hurt of that experience. But one good thing did come from it. I determined in my heart, to never do the same thing to another human being, especially a young person. For the most part I have kept that promise to myself and to the Lord. I decided to give people 'The Benefit of the Doubt', to believe the best about folks and not the worst. More than likely, I have had the wool pulled over my eyes a few times down through the years because of this philosophy, but that's okay. Life is better lived believing most people to be good, sincere and honest. I would much rather live that way than the alternative. People usually rise to the occasion and respond favorably when you treat them with respect and honor, believing the best about them rather than the worst and by giving them 'The Benefit of the Doubt'.

The Moth
(a lesson learned)

It was a beautiful September day in Texas. Tom and I had built a close friendship while attending college at Southwestern Assemblies of God University. After a month of daily talks over a very early breakfast, walking to classes together and late evening, after curfew visits from my dorm room window, we decided that we would actually go on a date with each other. Since we were both fond of Mexican food, the plan was to get some lunch at a local Dallas restaurant and then spend the rest of the day at Six Flags over Texas.

The day was actually rather warm, which is normal for this area, in the fall. We arrived at the restaurant on Colorado Blvd. at about eleven oclock. We were both a little tense, because our relationship up until that moment had been strictly friendship and now we were entering uncharted waters of new possibilities. It was a little silly to be apprehensive, because we had spent so many hours talking about almost everything, from our childhood to our vision for the future. Nevertheless, we were a bit nervous.

The restaurant was rather busy for a Saturday lunch hour. Most of the tables were occupied, and soon enough our waiter had seated us in a booth of our own. The decorations of huge tissue flowers and sombreros covered the walls and festive, colorful tablecloths and napkins adorned the tables. The Latino music was soft but lively and the droning voices and laughter of the crowd was at a tolerable level. Our conversation began fairly normally as we looked at our menus. After making our selections, I became a little subdued as I looked at this rather handsome man and realized that something special was growing between us. I hadn't planned on this at all. In fact, during my first year of college, I HAD been looking for a man to possibly be my husband. But this year, I had decided that my studies, my singing and my relationship with God would take priority. Men were near the bottom of my list of interests. Isn't it ironic that when you quit pushing the issue, things happen? Here was a man that had become my friend, one that I respected and admired. These thoughts were going through my mind, while I sat there listening to one of Tom's stories about his family and life in South Texas.

Before long, we had placed our order and the waiter brought our salad. We prayed and began to eat. I had begun to loosen up a bit and was talking easily with Tom when I noticed something was out of place. As I prepared to take another bite of my salad, in the midst of the lettuce, tomatoes, carrots and cabbage, I saw a huge moth in my bowl, covered with my favorite French dressing. I glanced up at Tom to see if he had noticed. He met my gaze evenly as I gave him a small smile. I didn't want anything to mar our special day together, so I decided just to lay my fork down and push the dish aside. I glanced down again to inspect the creature, hoping there weren't any missing parts. It appeared to be intact, which I was thankful for. I knew if Tom was aware of the moth, he would be embarrassed about it. However, my plan failed. I guess my disgust for the insect must have shown on my face and Tom knew immediately that something was amiss. He asked me what was wrong and I reluctantly showed him. His eyes grew large and he turned a little red. He kindly but firmly called for our waiter and showed him the unwanted, extra bit of protein that had been deposited in my salad. Of course the waiter was appalled and took the offensive bowl away from the table, alerting the manager to the situation. Apologies were made and an offer of a new salad was given. I decided that I would forego their kind suggestion, but we did decide to stay and finish the remainder of our meal. I was so proud of Tom and the way he handled everything. My respect for him grew even more that day. I was glad that he wasn't the kind of man who would lambast the staff and embarrass everyone. And I'm sure he was glad that I didn't dissolve into tears or go into hysterics because of the situation. Let's face facts, some people would have had that reaction. With the incident behind us, we continued on with our special date and thoroughly enjoyed our time together.

Now I know that some people might have vowed never to return to that particular restaurant again and perhaps they would even swear off Mexican food altogether. Some folks might have even seen the incident as a sign that maybe this relationship wasn't something to pursue. They could have read all sorts of negativity into the event, but what a shame that would have been. We enjoyed the rest of our meal (no more insects). We enjoyed the rest of our day filled with fun, silliness and lots of laughter. We even returned to that same restaurant many times, over the next few years and never encountered another moth.

Various individuals have a tendency to write off a restaurant, a relationship or even a church because of a negative experience. But let's face it, where people are involved there will be mistakes made whether in our personal world or in the church world. Let's try our best to put ourselves into the shoes of others, giving second and even third chances. Let's not miss out on special blessings and lifelong relationships because of misunderstandings or mistakes made.

Do I want another moth in my salad? Not really! But I am thankful for the incident that taught me these valuable lessons. It also helped me to gain some insight into the character of the man that I would one day marry. I'm grateful that I didn't take that incident as a negative indicator for our relationship. I could have missed out on many adventures, blessings and a deep abiding love that accompanied our marriage of forty years. Believe it or not, a moth in your salad can prove to be a blessing, if you let it!

Two Heads are Better Than One

It has been said that when a man and a woman get married, that the two become one flesh. Couples have a tendency to finish each other's sentences and seem to know what the other one is thinking. They complement one another, each using their own unique talents, gifts and strengths to handle a situation more completely. In our forty years of marriage, Tom and I found this to be true.

We met in the Spring of 1972, having been introduced to each other by Tom's roommate and my cousin, Jimmy. I was dating someone else at the time so the relationship didn't blossom right then. We didn't really become friends until the fall after returning from summer vacation. Over the summer one of our mutual friends, the guy I had been dating when we first met, had drown in a freak accident. I was very confused and had lots of questions about his death. It seemed so pointless. I decided that this semester I was going to concentrate on the Lord, my studies and my singing. 'There would be no room for guys or dating' I thought. I was determined that my spiritual and academic health would take priority.

But I wasn't the only one with questions. Tom was also searching for some semblance of meaning, in our friends passing. We started talking one day, sharing our memories and thoughts with each other. We began meeting at 6am for breakfast and then walking to our classes together. And although we didn't really come to any conclusions, the conversations helped us work through our questions and grief. We continued meeting like this for several days and then Tom wanted to talk in the evenings, but he didn't get off work until after my curfew. So, he would stand beneath my second floor window and throw pebbles against the glass. I opened the window and we would talk for about an hour. After several days, I got smart and hung a string out the window with a bell inside my room. This worked well until my roommates' boyfriends discovered our secret messaging system and also started using it. (You have to understand that this was in the days before cell phones or even private phones in the rooms. It was the early 70's, people!)

Before long, we were spending every spare minute together when we weren't in class, in the dorm or at work. People began teasing and making comments about a "relationship". But we just smiled and said "We're just friends". As friends, we ate together, went to classes, attended church, studied, and talked about everything. Before long, we realized that the teasing had substance and that our feelings for each other went deeper. We began talking about our vision of ministry and our dreams for the future. We found that we agreed on so many things and quite often would build on each other's ideas. So after about a month, we began dating. This led to hugs and flowers, hand-holding and sweet love notes, conversations about a life together and preparations to meet the parents.

One evening while driving back to the dorm, after one of our life planning sessions out at the lake, I mentioned to Tom the fact that he had never actually proposed to me. He smiled that quirky grin of his, and while keeping his left hand on the steering wheel, he reached for my hand and said, "Hey Sugar, will you marry me?" I smiled right back, squeezing his hand and said "Yes, I will". We continued on down the road quite content, a smile on our lips and my head on his shoulder.

After another week, we went ring shopping in Dallas and found the perfect ring at a little jewelry store on Jefferson Avenue, right down the street from my home church. Tom put some money down and made arrangements to pay weekly installments until it was paid for and he could put the ring on my finger.

Tom had already met my mom over Sunday dinner and a Dallas Cowboys football game on TV. He learned that day that our family were serious Cowboy fans. At some point during the game, he fell asleep on the couch. But that little nap didn't last long. As soon as Dallas made an exciting play, mom and I jumped up yelling and clapping our hands, which was quite normal for us. Tom jolted awake flying off the couch rather startled. Then when he realized what had happened, he looked at me strangely, shaking his head. I smiled at him, wondering at this man who would dare fall asleep during a Dallas Cowboys football game. Unbelievable!!

A couple of weeks later, my dad flew in for a weekend and took us out to dinner. He was determined to get to know this young man who had won my heart. The dinner and most of the weekend was spent talking, playing games, laughing and a little bit of interrogating. And through it all, we discovered that Tom and Dad had a lot in common and viewed life alike. Tom passed inspection with flying colors. Dad Approved!! .

I already knew Tom's older brother and sister in law, because he rented a room from them there at the college. Christmas came, and with the engagement ring firmly in place, I traveled to Brazoria to meet the rest of his family. I was to meet mom and dad and little sister Patsy. What a fun time we all had together.

After arriving and visiting for a while, I learned that their Christmas traditions were very different from what I was used to. Presents at the Behrend household were opened on Christmas Eve and there were no Christmas stockings. In my house and in my extended family, no presents were to be opened until Christmas day and Santa always filled the stockings when he came on Christmas morning.

And then something very unexpected happened. Early on Christmas morning when I awoke, I learned that Tom and his dad were not home. Did they go to do some last minute shopping?? No, because in those days, nothing was open on Christmas day. Were they called away on an emergency to help a neighbor or a friend? They were both very caring and always ready to lend a hand when it came to fixing things. To my way of thinking, it had to be something very important to be gone on Christmas morning. Where could they have gone?? What urgent task had pulled them away from their family?? Before long, I was informed that 'They had gone fishing'. This was beyond belief!! FISHING?? ON CHRISTMAS DAY?? This was on the verge of shocking for me. Almost beyond my comprehension! But everyone else in the house seemed unaffected by this occurrence, acting as if this was normal behavior. So I took a deep breath, calmed myself down and started helping with the preparations. While the men were gone, the women of the family had a very enjoyable time of working together, talking, laughing and making Christmas dinner.

By noon the men had returned with 27 reds and flounders, an amazing catch. I was happy for them and took a picture of Tom and his dad showing off their trophies. But then I learned something that caused my jaw to drop again. Mom was expected to clean the fish. "Now let me see if I understand this correctly", I thought. "The men had the fun and enjoyment of catching the fish and then she, the woman who had been working tirelessly on dinner, was expected to clean these fish?" Oh No, this could NOT be!! That's NOT fair!

However, Mom Behrend was perfectly happy doing this and did it without any complaining or grumbling.

Later on, when Tom and I were making plans for our life together, we discussed this arrangement. This was one area that we did not think alike and a compromise had to be found. After talking it over, we came to an agreement. If HE caught the fish, HE cleaned the fish. But I would willingly and happily help package, store and cook the creatures. Problem Solved!! In our later years, this arrangement also worked out well for deer, caribou and moose.

Tom and I didn't always see eye to eye on everything, but we were able to talk things through and figure out how to meet halfway. There weren't too many more fishing trips on Christmas morning, but a few. When celebrating Christmas in our own home we decided to open one or two presents on Christmas Eve and the rest on Christmas morning, much to the disappointment of our children, I might add, who preferred the Behrend tradition.

There were many other areas where we had to put our heads together and figure out a compromise that we were both happy with. For most of our married life, we both brought home paychecks but I had the responsibility of paying the bills. I took care of the house but if we were both working full time jobs, Tom would help out. The cooking was usually my job, but Tom would pitch in when needed. He took care of the vehicles, the yard and repairs. We discussed and planned any major purchases, but minor ones weren't an issue. If working late or going to lunch with a friend, we called each other. Communication was the key.

At family gatherings, Tom would focus in on one person at a time, finding out how they were truly doing, talking at length and sharing stories. I would survey the room trying to make sure everyone was being taken care of, had something to drink and visiting briefly with each one. Most of the time, Tom would lead in our Bible and prayer time, but sometimes he would want me to. In ministry, Tom focused on preaching and teaching to the adults. I focused on the worship and ministry to the younger generation. He would handle phone calls and meetings with people while I would take care of the administrative organization and office work.

It's amazing to me now, when I look back, how we complimented each other with our abilities in different areas. God truly knew what He was doing when He brought us together. Between the two of us, we pretty much covered all the needs. And through the years, as we considered what was best and where each of our talents lay, we learned how to work together even more. And as we each gave up some of 'our rights' and began to think of the other person more than ourselves, love grew even stronger and we found that things just seemed to work better.

We found that 'two heads were definitely better than one' especially when they are both committed to God and to each other.

God Works in Mysterious Ways Indeed

Life was good but busy. Tom was going to Bible college full time and working full time at Larkin Machine shop in the evenings. I worked at Southwestern Bell and was concentrating on being a good wife and hoping to be a mother someday soon. We attended, supported and worked in Tom's brother's church in Maypearl, Texas. After eighteen months of marriage, things seemed to be progressing well. Life was in a steady routine.

THEN THE PAIN BEGAN. Tom would come home early from work because he was having severe pain in various areas of his body but mostly in the legs, knees and ankles. At first, it was occasional but started happening more frequently. Leaving work early or not even going in started happening more often. He began going to doctors to try to find answers. They ran all kinds of tests trying to locate the source of the ache. A couple of doctors accused him of faking so he could get on disability and not have to work. This was very disturbing and upsetting, because Tom was a firm believer in hard work. Even a close friend that labored with him and attended the same Bible collage berated him for his lack of faith. However, a doctor in Grand Prairie believed Tom to be sincere. He put him in the hospital for a nine day stay, running every kind of test he could think of, but still there were no answers.

After six months of trying to push through the pain and continue life as usual, going to college and working, the roof caved in. Tom had to be escorted from work one evening because he was unable to walk out by himself. He was in such severe agony that he could no longer stand up and do his machinist job. That's when he made the decision to quit working, quit college, quit volunteer work at the church, quit preaching and concentrate on finding answers. At the age of 23, Tom applied for disability and was quickly accepted.

The next year was spent in and out of doctor's offices. There were two more ten day stays at hospitals with numerous tests. And then finally, at Scott and White Diagnostic Hospital in Temple Texas, the doctors discovered the problem. Tom was diagnosed with Inflammatory Arthritis. We were sent home with the news that there was no cure and he could only manage this disease and torture by taking twelve aspirins every day, for the rest of his life.

During this year, we had spent many days and nights seeking answers from the Lord and much prayer went up for Tom. We attended services held by big healing evangelists and stood in more than one prayer line, which was very hard on him. During all this, we never saw a difference even though we tried to do everything right and according to God's Word. We were in survival mode. When the diagnosis was given, it seemed that we were hurled into a dark pit of despair and hopelessness. But despite the raging battle, we desperately continued to hold on to God and His Word.

And then one day, a couple of months after the diagnosis, we attended a service at our little home church in Maypearl. Tom had to use crutches to get around and was in the process of getting a wheelchair because the pain and loss of muscle mass had escalated. This particular service was to be led by an evangelist preacher, and even though Tom didn't feel well, we attended. Since the church was so small, we wanted to show our support. When the preacher began, neither of us was very impressed with his preaching or his appearance. He was twenty years behind the times in his dress and had a front tooth missing. But we sat obediently until the end of the service, anxious to get home after the final prayer. However, things didn't go as we planned. Praise God! This preacher was intent on having a prayer service and started calling people down to pray for them as he felt the Lord leading. My husband was afraid that he would call on him and sure enough he did. Tom started to refuse but didn't want to make a scene or embarrass his brother, who was the pastor of the church. As the man brought him forward and began to pray for him, he laid hands on him, touching each area that was affected by the disease: both ankles, the right knee, the left hip, the lower back, the left shoulder and the right jaw. God Almighty directed this plain, back-woods country preacher to pray for ONLY those areas that were affected and painful.

Tom was not healed that night but he was filled with faith and a renewed hope. He knew without a shadow of a doubt that God was in control and that his healing was coming.

A few weeks later, Tom developed a sore throat and went to the doctor. They gave him antibiotics to clear up the infection. After taking a couple of doses, he realized that he could move better and that the pain had diminished. As he took the medication, he was able to do things he hadn't done in months. He called his arthritis doctor, telling him about what was happening. After some research, the doctor informed us that sometimes bad teeth or tonsils can cause this disease. After an examination, the doctor suggested that Tom have his tonsils removed as soon as possible.

So once again we headed back to Scott and White Diagnostic Hospital, for a surgery this time. But this trip was very different from the other visits because we had the assurance that God had everything under control. After the procedure, all of Toms' symptoms were gone. The only pain he had was from the operation. There was no discomfort or stiffness in any of the joints or muscles that had been plaguing him for eighteen months. He no longer had arthritis. His recovery was complete, never suffering with that disease again. He was able to go back to Bible College, resume working full time and started preaching again.

Praise the Lord for His keeping power, His healing and provision. God had given us a miracle in his own miraculous manner and instance.

The ways and timing of the Lord are truly amazing and mysterious!!

Mothers

I have been blessed in my life to know and be loved by some amazing mothers. Of course at the top of my list is my own mom, Reba. I guess when you grow up with a wonderful mother, you somehow expect that all children are also blessed in this way. After a few years you realize that some moms fall short, some are negligent and selfish, thinking of themselves before their children. But most moms are thoughtful, hard-working, kind and loving. And when you grow up with a great mother, you don't grasp the blessing of such a lady until a little later in your years when your eyes are opened to the realities of life. My mom was a great mom, not because she was exceptionally talented or beautiful, but because she was a woman of excellence and strong faith. She WAS talented and She WAS beautiful. She was considerate, thoughtful and generous. She was so open and giving, always ready to do without in order to bless someone else, usually me. She was hard-working and pretty much raised me alone after my parents' divorce when I was nine. She made sure I was involved in every church and school activity even though she was exhausted after a full day at work as an executive secretary. And although she had her faults, they were insignificant because of the great many positive traits that she displayed on a daily basis. She didn't see the beauty in herself, she thought herself boring, but she wasn't. She was delightful to be around. Her joyous laughter and the clapping of her hands when one of the kids or grandkids did something cute, was so much fun to watch. She got so excited when a deserving person on a game show won a nice prize, you would have thought that she was the winner. She was so smart, usually beating me at guessing the puzzle on Wheel of Fortune but she would never rub it in or boast. Everyone who knew her, loved her, especially her daughter.

I knew that kids in her neighborhood loved her and would go to her with their problems, needs or even if they just needed a snack. It wasn't until after her death in 2010 that I heard an amazing story about her. She had provided food and support for three little girls who lived next door to her. For about four months, they would come over daily 'to spend time' with her, usually eating a sandwich and using the bathroom facilities. They would ask her to wash their clothes because 'their washer was broke' and their mom didn't have time to get it fixed. She noticed that she rarely saw the mom come or go but the girls always had an excuse as to why mom was gone. She continued helping these young girls, ages 8, 9 and 11, taking them into her home whenever needed. For a while, they stayed with her at night. The girls had told her that their mom had to go out of town for a few days and my mom didn't want them to be alone in the house. After a few months, the truth finally came out. The mother was staying elsewhere most of the time and hadn't paid the electric bill, so they had no power. Mother continued to help these girls until finally some of their family stepped in to rescue them and remedy the situation. The girls, now grown with children of their own, had kept in touch with her through the years and were heart-broken when she died. They credited her with saving their lives during that time. I indeed had a wonderful and exceptional mother.

My second mother came into my life when I was about ten years old, after my parent's divorce. Betty was the kind of stepmom that anyone would be blessed to have. She always had hugs for me and a special smile when she called me 'dahlin'. She understood the pain that I was dealing with at my separation from my daddy and tried to love me through it. She never treated me like a stepchild but included me whenever possible. That's one of the reasons that I call her my second mom. She was so much better than a stepmom and how that word is interpreted. She consistently spoke and showed her love for me, allowing me to help with dinner or letting me help around the house. She trusted me to help take care of my little sister when she was born, allowing me to babysit and do whatever was needed. She was an incredible cook, making the simplest dish taste amazing. She taught me how to prepare certain foods, sharing her delicious and special recipes. She would divulge her insights and secrets to cleaning and taking care of a home. But most of all, I saw how she treated my daddy. She took really good care of him and made him very happy. And it was evident that they loved each other deeply. She was an extraordinary woman of faith and prayer and I loved her dearly and cherish the relationship that we had.

The third mother to come into my life, arrived on my wedding day. Melvine became my mother-in-law and accepted me as one of her own. I learned of her loving and caring nature at the beginning. She was tireless in her sincere determination to try and take care of everyone who came through her door. She was a superb cook and housekeeper, always greeting people with a smile and a listening ear. I knew that I was considered one of the family, because I was always included in preparations and even asked my opinion.

There were a couple of times through the years when Tom and I had to live with Mom and Dad Behrend for a short time. During those days and weeks, I discovered first hand that she was a prayer warrior, who took her family and friends to the throne of God before the break of day, every morning. She loved praise and worship music and had it playing on her television or radio throughout the day. She was always prepared to listen to your problems and pray for any need.

So you see, I was supremely blessed throughout my life with wonderful, Godly moms. Don't get me wrong, they each had their faults and failings but ultimately they were all women of integrity, faith, honor and beauty. I truly hope that the same can be said of me someday.

I Am Loved
(and so are you)

Have you ever walked into a store, church or a restaurant and unexpectedly run into a friend or acquaintance. When they see you, their face lights up, they smile and wave, until you respond by coming over to them for a hug or a handshake. How does that make you feel? Doesn't it give you a warm glow, a feeling of acceptance, a realization that someone is glad to see you and to know you? Doesn't it make your day a little brighter and your step a little lighter? Of course it does. We all need to know that we are loved and appreciated, that someone is glad to see us. Believe it or not that is just how God feels about us. He is overjoyed when we walk into the room especially if we have come to see Him and to spend some time with Him.

Let me tell you how I know this to be true. Of course, the Word of God is full of accounts of God's great love for us and is displayed in many of the great stories of the Bible. But the Lord honored me in 1999 with first-hand knowledge of this truth that shall stay with me forever and I want to share it with you.

That year, I worked at Dayspring Christian Academy as a teacher's assistant. That particular Wednesday was like any other. We started the school day with classes and then came together for a chapel service. The principal, Dianne Logan, was leading worship. There was an extraordinary presence of God in the chapel that morning and at one point she encouraged us to close our eyes and individually enter into God's presence to worship Him. As I obeyed, it seemed that I was transported to heaven. I saw the throne room before me. Such a brilliant white with a golden glow all around and yet it didn't hurt my eyes. I remember thinking that it was so beautiful, I could hardly take it in. As I walked forward, I could see a raised platform before me with two thrones. There were two men seated in flowing brilliant robes. They were talking and laughing happily, the one on the left leaning toward the other. I instinctively knew that the Father was on my right and Jesus on my left. I had intended to come before the Lord and bow down to worship Him. I felt no fear or trepidation, just reverent awe and determined purpose as I slowly came forward. As I continued to draw near, Jesus turned and saw me. He knew my intention immediately. When our eyes met, His face lit up with such pure joy that I felt consumed by the waves of love that washed over me. He was happy, no, He was thrilled, no, He was ecstatic that I had chosen to come to see Him and spend time with Him. Me, little ole me, on the receiving end of such an intense, adoring gaze. I started to fall to my knees in thankful adoration, but He hurried down the steps from His throne and caught me before I could kneel. He wrapped me in His arms and held me in a tender yet firm embrace. I laid my head on His shoulder and melted into His chest letting His love surround and engulf me.

The peace and adoration that I felt in that one moment was incredible. Such a realization was almost too much to bear. I knew in that instance that I was adored, important and cherished.

AND SO ARE YOU!! Take hold of this truth, SO ARE YOU!!

Our Lord sees the beauty in us, the potential in us, the purpose for which we were created, the unique giftings in each of us. He sees to the very depth of who we are and to Him it is beauty personified. Many times, we don't see these things in ourselves. We know our strengths and weaknesses. We know where we fail and where we excel. We are so good at looking at our flaws rather than our good points. And let's face it, the enemy plays tricks with our mind, making us focus on the negative rather than the positive. But let's not listen to the father of lies, let's listen to the lover of our soul. Let's seek Him out and allow His love and truth to speak to us. I encourage you to do as I have done, go to Him during your very busy day. Find your quiet place, that precious closet of intimacy with Him. Enter into His throne room reverently and humbly. Then you too will come away feeling cherished and adored, because let's face it, YOU ARE cherished and adored.

Reflections in Colorado

Reflections in Concrete

Greeley or Mom (God's Way or my way)

In 1977, Tom graduated from Southwestern Assembly of God University with his Bachelor of Science degree in Christian Ministry. I came away with two years of college and no official degree but did obtain my MRS. Degree when Tom and I got married. After his graduation, we were invited to come to Glad Tidings Assembly of God in Greeley Colorado as Youth Ministers under Pastors Nelson and Betty Bascom.

When Tom first told me of his desire to go to Colorado, I was not very enthusiastic. Yes, it was a beautiful state full of many wonders and incredible sites. I had thoroughly enjoyed our honeymoon there, a few years earlier. But it was a full days drive from Dallas and my mom, and that was unimaginable to me. I remember thinking "It's too far away from my mom". I had never been that distance from home and my mother for more than a few weeks at a time. How could he ask me to go such a far distance away from her to LIVE? She was alone and I was her only child. We had always been close in so many ways. Surely this was not a part of God's plan.

At first I dismissed the idea, thinking it was just a whim and that he would get over it. But as Tom talked and dreamed out loud, I could see that this was something very important to him, so I decided that <u>maybe</u> I should pray about it, and I did. When we drove up to Greeley to see the church and check into this position, I was still praying and unsure. I had decided to enjoy our time away and to treat it as a vacation. But after meeting the Bascoms and the people at the church, I knew that this was God's plan for our lives. Although we had never met these people, when we were with them, it felt like we were at home. Somehow it was just Right! God had given me clear direction. So I relented and prepared to break the news to my mom. Of course, she was disappointed that we would be so far away, but she was such a trooper and encouraged us to follow God's will for our lives. Little did I know that six years down the road I would be seeking the Lord again. And again, I would be repeating that phrase "But it's too far away from my mom". This time Tom expressed his desire to move to Alaska. But in that instance also, when I opened my heart and mind to the Lords leading, He gave me clear direction.

Our time in Greeley with Nelson, Betty and Dianne was invaluable in preparing us for our future ministry in all the various places and situations that we would encounter. The Bascoms became family to us. We were accepted into their home and hearts as precious children. We learned the art of hospitality in this loving home and the meals that were served, were fit for a king. Then we would laugh together as we shared stories or played games. They were people of exceptional character and Godliness. They each taught us so much and allowed Tom and I to stretch, try new things, make mistakes and learn from them without condemnation. Toms preaching, teaching and counseling skills were honed and fine-tuned. I learned how to talk and interact with people more comfortably. My musical skills were appreciated and inspired to new levels. The encouragement and teaching that we received was soaked in and stored away. Many of the lessons that we learned would be used over and over again down through the years to come. The closeness that was nurtured would last for a lifetime.

What if I had been stubborn and had refused to leave my mom. What if I had insisted on having my own way, declined to step into the unknown and get out of my comfort zone. What a shame it would have been to miss out on the wonderful years of friendship, mentoring, teaching and empowerment.

I've been told that 'Life is short, take a risk'. That statement is SO true. I've heard others say that it's the things we don't take a risk for that we end up regretting. I have also found this to be true. What happens if you try something and it fails? You pick yourself up and try something else, but at least you ventured forth. I've also heard the story of Walt Disney applying for a job as a cartoonist for a newspaper and being told that his drawings and ideas didn't show any imagination. What if he had listened to those naysayers and had quit trying? What a loss that would have been for millions of people.

How much more imperative is it for us, as Christians, to follow God's leading? It is vitally important for possibly millions of people and can affect their lives eternally. I'm thankful that God put Greeley Colorado and the people there in my life. Yes, it led me away from my precious mother but I know that it was a good decision that she is also proud that I made. Maybe millions have not been affected for eternity because of that decision but there are possibly thousands that have.

I am thankful to my Lord and Savior for His leading and all He has done in us. I am also thankful for Nelson, Betty and Dianne Bascom(Logan) and for all the incredible years of teaching, mentoring, loving, encouraging, friendship and Godly examples. What a difference you have made in so many lives, but especially in the lives of Tom and Vonnie Behrend.

The Tie

I have entered a few contests over the years. I use to think that somehow Publishers Clearing House would surely show up at my door someday. For a while, I believed that a person could actually win something substantial at one of those carnival games or could get a nice stuffed animal with those machines with the claw that reaches down to grab your prize. But, I have long ago come to the realization that I may as well flush my money down the toilet rather than play these games, because the outcome is the same, nothing, nada, zilch!!

However, there was one instance when I did get the chance to win a prize in a contest that I entered. In 1979, a $100 gift certificate for any store at the mall, was a nice prize. I decided to go for it. The contest was called "The Ugliest Tie Contest". Anyone could submit a necktie to be judged by a panel and if it was determined to be the ugliest tie, you would win. In those days, ties were quite popular and Tom had quite a few. I thought that surely one of his ties would qualify for this prize. But as I went through his closet, none of them really jumped out at me. To be honest, when we bought ties for him, we tried to get attractive and trendy neckware. I picked out one or two that I thought might make the cut but didn't really think they were ugly enough.

So I started my quest for the ugliest tie, going to garage sales, resale shops and 2nd hand stores. The deadline for turning in your tie entry was soon approaching. I had been searching everywhere for about two weeks. The Saturday of the deadline, I went back to one of the resale shops that I had visited before and THERE IT WAS. The tie was a tan and brown color on the back and around the edges. But in the middle, there was a hand painted scene of a fisherman standing in a stream. He had cast his line out and on the end of it, he had caught this huge, ugly, blue and red fish. I knew I had found THE TIE. I paid my 25 cents and happily left the store, confident in my purchase. At least, I was confident until I got back home and showed it to Tom. He thought it was great and liked the tie. He was impressed with the quality of the silky material and the attention to detail that the artist had put into the painting of the stream, fish and fisherman.

He knew about my quest to find an ugly tie and really didn't think that this one would win, but I was out of time so I decided to submit it anyway. No longer was I confident that I had this win "in the bag" because now I had seen it through someone else's eyes. I looked past the initial ugliness and began to see an inner beauty that I hadn't noticed before. What would the judges see, the ugliness or the beauty? I submitted my entry and waited. The results wouldn't come out for a week. The following Saturday, a friend of mine from church called me on the phone to offer her congratulations. I had won the contest! I went down to the mall and collected my $100 gift certificate but they wanted to keep the tie for another week to display with the runners up. In many ways, it WAS an ugly tie but also it was uniquely beautiful. After I retrieved it from the mall, I gave it to my husband. He did wear it, proudly, a few times through the years. But he always chose those occasions carefully when he knew that we would be with people who would appreciate the humor of the story and the uniqueness of tie.

Doesn't this remind you of how God looks at us? Other people may look at someone and totally miss their beauty. In many cases, circumstance or life in general can give the appearance of ugliness. But if we will look at others through God's eyes, we will see the unique beauty that is there. Each of us bear both ugliness and beauty at some point in our lives. What will we choose to see in those around us? Will we only look at the surface? Or will we choose to look more closely and deeply? I hope that I will always follow God's example.

Sledding and Boulders Don't Mix

A Colorado mountain covered in evergreen trees and pure white snow is a most beautiful and breathtaking sight. It was Christmas time 2002, and our friends from Brazoria, Texas had traveled all the way up to Glenwood Springs Colorado to spend the holidays with us. They actually came between Christmas and New Years while the kids were out of school. After arriving, we made plans for several fun activities together, activities not possible in south Texas.

First, we went skating at an outdoor, covered ice rink and enjoyed watching the kids as they learned how to maneuver on the ice. They were all bundled up from head to toe, so even when they did fall, they had lots of padding to absorb the shock. While there, we drank some of the best hot chocolate ever made or maybe it was just the chill in the air that made it seem so satisfying and tasty.

Next, we took everyone to the Glenwood outdoor Hot Springs pool, swimming in 30 degree, snowy weather. But since the pool was about 105 degrees, the only chilly, uncomfortable part of this outing, was going from the changing rooms to the pool. Once in the pool, you were toasty warm, able to float on your back catching falling snowflakes on your tongue, Oooo! Ahhh!

We also visited Sunlight Ski Slope where the kids and some of the adults enjoyed skiing and snowboarding. My daughter Angela and two of her friends, Stacy and Chelsea, all being between the ages of 11 and 14, took skiing lessons from a rather attractive, French ski instructor. He was quite charming and had the girls blushing and giggling throughout the lessons. I think that the girls were a little disappointed when their instruction time was ended and they had to try out their newfound knowledge on the slopes without him there to assist them.

I, on the other hand was perfectly content watching everyone as they came down the mountain, taking candid pictures and drinking thick, steaming, whipped crème topped, hot chocolate. Mmmm. I had learned many years ago, when in my early 30's that snow skis and I didn't get along. That outing didn't turn out to be as pleasant as this one was shaping up to be. That day consisted of a twisted knee that landed me in bed for about three weeks. So I was quite happy to forego the 'fun' and be the official photographer. It was a beautiful, joy-filled day with lots of laughter and just a few minor mishaps.

And then, we made plans for a sledding trip. Our church family from Glenwood Springs had a tradition of sledding down a certain hill not too far away from the Ski resort each year. Everyone would bring food and hot drinks, inner tubes and inflatables, and a couple of snow machines. Usually this event happened on New Years Day and this year was no different. We all loaded up into several vehicles taking all of our winter gear and equipment up the mountain. Right before going up the last road to the sledding hill, we stopped at a parking area with a port-a-potty. We were hoping to make use of this one and not have to go potty again until the trip home, because up on the hill there would only be a pile of snow to hide behind. Pam, Lillian, me and the girls went to the snow-encrusted little building to take care of business. But when we opened the door, we found a toilet seat piled with about 6" of snow and ice. Looking up we realized why. There was no roof on the frozen outhouse. Let's just say it was a chilly experience but served its purpose.

After everyone had a turn in the icy potty house, we went on up the last hill. We parked in a large secure area and built a bonfire with the wood we had brought along.

Then the men started the trip up the mountainside on the snowmobiles creating a sledding path for us to come down. The snow was quite deep, about 3 feet. The men traveled up and down the mountain several times to prepare the snow for the inner tubes. Then, here came the first sledding team on a 3 person inflatable. With each pass down the hill, the path was packed down a little more and the trip downhill became a little swifter. Laughter and screams of delight filled the air. People had snow ball fights while waiting for their turn up the mountain. Kids were chasing each other and cold snow being stuffed down the backs of coats became the newest game.

Lillian decided to teach these southern kids how to make a snow angel. This was a fun game for her until Gerry, one of the men from our church, decided to stuff snow up her pant leg while she squealed and helplessly tried to get up and away from his cold prank. She was quite outraged that her husband and her friends didn't come to her rescue. We truly considered helping but couldn't because we were laughing too hard. And then, everyone gathered around the fire drinking a hot beverage and warming their hands.

Finally, it was time for Lillian and I to go up the mountain on the snowmobile. Pam declined going up, choosing to warm up inside one of the trucks with the heat on full blast. We had decided that we wanted to come down on an inflatable together. So up, up, up we went. From the bottom it didn't look that far, but from the top it seemed much further. However, we were committed now and everyone else had enjoyed a wonderful time on their turn. Lillian sat on the front with her feet dangling over and I sat on the back. I had intended to sit up so I could see where we were going and wave to everyone as we came down. But as we began our descent, I fell back with my head and shoulders hanging off the top of the sled. And then we began to turn round and round and round, making white donuts in the snow. All I could see was blue sky with splashes of white snow flying all around. There was no controlling this crazy thing! We were laughing and screaming, not sure where we would end up. The spinning action of the sled caused us to veer off course from the carefully prepared path. Without realizing what was happening, we were headed straight for a huge boulder that stood up out of the snow about four feet. People at the bottom and the top could see what was happening but no one could do anything but pray. If Lillian's legs hit the boulder they would break and if my head hit the boulder, I could die. When we did hit, we were still laughing hysterically, still not realizing the imminent danger that we were in. But God intervened and the side of the inflatable hit the boulder and we were both thrown into the deep snow next to the huge rock. Our mouths filled up with snow, so for a few moments everything was quiet until sputtering and spitting we regained our breath and began laughing again. About a hundred feet below where we landed, our husbands were running up the hill through the deep snow trying to get to us. Our screams and laughter of delight sounded like screams of pain and injury to them, so they frantically made their way up the hill. When they reached us, Lillian's husband David, grabbed her by the shoulders, pulling her up out of the snow. He shook her frantically asking over and over "Lillian are you alright?" He had to ask her repeatedly because we were both laughing so hard that we couldn't speak. Finally, we were able to assure everyone that we were okay. A snowmobile came rushing down the mountain but we were able to walk the rest of the way to our friends and family.

Lillian and I decided that perhaps it would be best to forego any further sledding trips that day. Cold and wet from our wild, crazy adventure, we stood by the bonfire drinking hot chocolate and thanking the Lord for His protection and keeping power. And every now and then, we would look up that hill to the huge boulder sticking up out of the snow. We realized in that moment that our God was ever attentive and watching over us, even when we didn't know that we were in danger. That mountain could have been marred by tragedy that day, but because of God's protection and His goodness, it remained a beautiful, awe-inspiring sight, to be enjoyed again on another bright, beautiful and snowy day.

Marine to the Core

It was January 2006. Tom, Angela and I had flown into San Diego California the night before. We had settled into our hotel room, anxious for this special day. What an unbelievably beautiful place this was. We awoke to 75 degree weather, bright sunshine and blue skies. There were palm trees swaying and a sweet aroma of flowers floating on a gentle breeze. It was a perfect day to be outside witnessing the activities of our son, Judah, as he began the preliminaries of graduation from boot camp. We were all excited but especially Tom and I. For us, this was a day filled with a deep sense of pride and joy.

Judah had grown up playing with his G.I. Joes. He had a deep sense of duty and responsibility for helping and protecting others. He was taught to respect and honor fire-fighters, those in law enforcement and the military. His PawPaw, my dad, had been in the Army for many years and had retired a Lieutenant Colonel. Judah looked up to him and without our realizing it, he had at some point, decided to follow in his Grandpa's footsteps.

Judah informed us of his decision to join the Marines when he was about to graduate from high school. Our thought was, "Why the Marines? They are some of the first ones to go inland right into the middle of danger. Why not the Air Force or the Navy? They didn't usually get too close to the action, at least not right away." Judah informed us that he didn't want to be stuck on a ship for six months at a time. "But the Marines?" we thought. Judah didn't have a mean bone in his body. He was a kind, considerate and compassionate man like Tom. If a person hurt and cried, Judah would sit with them and hurt and cry also. He cared so much about people. Marines had to be really hard and mean, didn't they? Anyway, that's what we thought at the time. But Judah had his mind made up. He made an appointment for a marine recruiter to come to our house and try to sell us on the idea. Tom and I really didn't want to go down this road, but Judah was almost grown and so we decided to hear him out. The recruiter came and spent about three hours with us, telling us all the positive things about military life and extolling the virtues of being a marine. He made all kinds of promises about Judah being able to choose his own duty assignments and the many benefits of signing up. After he left, we had a long and serious talk. Tom and I weren't convinced that this was the right time. We told Judah that we would prefer that he went to college for a couple of years and then revisit the idea, if he was still interested. He reluctantly but obediently agreed to our request.

The first year, Judah lived at home while working for Coca Cola and attending a local community college. He was able to get some basic courses under his belt. He was very careful to save his money during that year and was able to go off to college the next year. He attended Masters Commission in Phoenix Arizona during that second year. It proved to be a wonderful and inspiring time for him. However, two weeks before coming home, at the end of the school year, he revisited the Marine Corp idea. This time, he didn't hesitate to sign on the dotted line. Before he arrived home from college, he informed us of what he had done. How could we argue? He had given college a chance and his dream of being a Marine still burned deep inside. He had to follow his heart.

So here we were, the day before graduation, waiting to see our son who had been gone from home for about four months. Our correspondence and phone calls had been sparse. When he left home he had weighed about 180 and now he was down to 150. Boot Camp had been a brutal experience, as we knew it would be. But our loving, kind son had endured and had become stronger than he could have ever imagined. Strong in many ways. The drill instructors had thrown everything at them to make them into the hearty, tough soldiers that they now were. Judah had told us a few things that had happened but I know he spared me from knowing too many details. He had persevered and we were beyond proud.

Now as the recruits began their final run, we strained our necks trying to find him among all of these young men. They ran in formation, but there were several units. And to be quite honest, they all looked alike. Everyone had similar builds, wore green shorts and t-shirts, and were bald. Where was he? We went to a different vantage point for the next lap around the parade grounds but still couldn't find him. Then we went to the area where they would end up and stand in formation. We were informed as to the unit he was in and where they would stand, so that narrowed it down some. When at last they stood in formation, it still took us several minutes to scan the faces with our telephoto camera lens to find him. I was beginning to wonder if he was actually there or had he been injured and was in the hospital or something. But No, finally we spotted him. He was standing very straight, full of pride and so still. We moved through the crowd so that we could stand nearer to him. We tried waving to gain his attention, but he stood resolute and strong, barely blinking an eye. The comments by his superiors seemed to take much too long. We were so anxious to speak to him and be able to give the first of many hugs in several months. Finally the speeches ended and the men were released to their families. Judah looked our way, smiled in his old familiar manner and moved into our joyful arms.

The remainder of the day was spent talking, laughing and catching up on everything as he showed us around the base and introduced us to several of his new friends. Later that evening, we went back to our hotel and Judah returned to his barracks to prepare for the graduation ceremonies the following day.

The sun was shining brightly the next morning. Again, the palm trees waved peacefully in the light ocean breeze as we drove back to the base for the special event we were to participate in. However, this time, bleachers had been constructed, flags fluttered crisply in the wind, an excellent and pristine military band played flawlessly and the soldiers were decked out in their finest uniforms. It was a perfect day for such a memorable and special moment. Parents, family and friends filtered into the stands, snapping pictures and taking videos of everything. Announcements were made and then the band began to play as the Marines marched across the field and halted in perfect formation. This time we were able to find Judah more quickly and proceeded to take numerous pictures as each company of men were presented for graduation. Judah stood tall, strong and was so handsome. And we stood tall, strong and were so proud. I have a feeling that my dad was able to watch from the portals of heaven as his grandson honored him by following in his footsteps. Our son had a dream and a vision for his future. He had honored us by trying our way first and then had pursued his own calling. Judah had certainly earned the title of Marine and was a Marine to the core.

SING TO THE KiNG

Vs.1 Sing to the King Who is coming to reign, Glory to Jesus, the Lamb that was slain.   Life and salvation His empire shall bring, Joy to the nations when Jesus is King.

Chorus: Come let us sing a song, a song declaring, we belong to Jesus, He's all we need. Lift up a heart of praise, sing now with voices raised to Jesus, Sing to the King.

Vs.2 For His returning we watch and we pray, we will be ready the dawn of that day. We'll join in singing with all the redeemed, satan is vanquished and Jesus is King.

COME, NOW IS THE TIME TO WORSHP

Come, now is the time to worship. Come, now is the time to give your heart.   Come, just as you are to worship.
Come, just as you are before your God, come.

Lord, One day every tongue will confess You are God.
One day every knee will bow.   Still the greatest treasure
remains for those who gladly choose You now.

AMAZING GRACE (my chains are gone)

Vs. 1 Amazing grace how sweet the sound that saved a wretch like me
I once was lost but now I'm found, was blind but now I see.

Vs. 2 Twas grace that taught my heart to fear & grace my fears relieve
how precious did that grace appear the hour I first believed.

Chorus: My chains are gone, I've been set free. My God, my Savior ha
ransomed me. And like a flood His mercy reigns, unending love, amazing grace.

Vs. 3 The Lord has promised good to me, His Word my hope secures.
He will my shield and pardon be, as long as life endures.

Vs. 4 The earth shall soon dissolve like snow, the sun forbear to shine,
But God who called us here below shall be forever mine.

Reflections in Alaska

Hidden Beauty in a Frozen and Barren Land

In December of 1983, Tom and I moved from Denver Colorado to Alaska. We were to serve as associate pastors at my brother-in-laws church in Bethel. We started the process to sell our house and cars. And even though the process of liquidating our things didn't seem to be progressing, we firmly believed that we were in the will of God. Some of our family tried to discourage us from moving so far away. In fact, Tom's mom believed and told us that if this move was truly in God's plan, then our house would sell. We were taking a huge leap of faith. We decided to move forward with our plans. We put many of our possessions in storage, filled our suitcases then packed and sent the rest of our belongings through the mail. As it worked out, we signed the final papers for the sale of the house on our way to board the airplane for our move to Alaska.

Flying into Anchorage had been an interesting and rather pleasant experience. The beautiful snow covered mountains and the lovely, modern city were welcome sights. We stayed the night there then left the next day for Bethel. It was late afternoon and had begun snowing by the time we took off. The snow covered scenery below was swallowed up by the early darkness of winter in the Arctic. We noticed that after about fifteen minutes in the air, we no longer saw any lights below us. Surely there were many towns along the 400 mile journey. Even though the weather had cleared, each time we looked out the window, we were greeted with only blackness. This was so alien to us. In the lower 48, there were towns every 40 – 50 miles. If it had been daylight, we would have realized that Alaska was truly a state of vast expanses of wilderness. The two hour trip was uneventful. As we started our descent into Bethel, we anxiously looked out the window to view our new home. However, we were unable to see anything, there were only a few lights visible. Surely we were on the outskirts of town and the lights were on the other side of the plane.

Upon landing, reality set in. We were actually on the very edge of the earth, far, far away from normal civilization. Our hearts sank and Tom began to silently scold himself for bringing us to this desolate place. The town possessed about two dozen street lights and two stop lights or so it seemed. Even though we didn't see any igloos, the houses were a simple frame build and many seemed elevated off the ground. As we passed the police station, we saw the only tree in sight. Everywhere we looked, there were huge snow drifts where the ever- blowing wind had piled it. Surely the morning light would reveal some redeeming qualities. After all, this was Alaska, a land filled with awe-inspiring beauty.

The morning revealed a frozen, inhospitable, windswept community. There were no mountains or trees only frozen and barren tundra covered with homes, a hospital, businesses, schools and churches. Even the snow held no element of fun because of the extreme cold. There were no snow men or snowball fights since the snow was so fine and powdery that it wouldn't hold together. But the icy particles did have a tendency of sneaking into your boots or coat. It would also slip under doors because of the constant wind. It seemed that this desolate place would only promise misery and at first we were certain that this was to be true for us.

But the places or surroundings where you are destined to live, can be survived and even relished if you trust God and keep an open mind. It also helps tremendously when the people there are folks of honor, humor and friendship. This is what we found in Bethel. Our new friends opened their hearts and homes to us. Friendships and close bonds were formed that would last a lifetime.

After a few weeks, we settled into a routine. Upon rising, we would find the water pipe that had frozen during the night. Usually, it was by the back door where the wind had found a tiny hole to sneak in. We would use a blow dryer to thaw it out so that we would have water for the day. We were able to find the frozen pipe because the water pipes ran on the inside of the house where you could see them, not inside of the walls. There was also an arctic entryway where we hung up coats and took off boots. In this area there was a huge 500 gallon tank where water would be delivered twice a week. So that meant that showers and baths were rationed and planned very carefully. Toilets were not flushed after every use either. I quickly learned the saying, "If it's yellow, let it mellow but if it's brown, flush it down". And then after about a month, we discovered that the sewer system sometimes froze up and we became acquainted with "honey buckets". I was so glad that part of my responsibility was not to remove the bucket and empty it outside in honey bucket lake or set it aside to freeze until spring when it could be emptied. We had wondered why we saw so many 5 gallon buckets on the conveyor belt at the airport. We realized quickly that they were a valuable commodity in this unusual place. This was certainly a very different way of life.

Going to work each morning entailed a lengthy process of many layers of clothing. I worked at the church daycare which was not too far away, only about 100 yards. But at -30 and 30 mph winds, you made sure that you were bundled up thoroughly. Pants, long-johns, two shirts, two pair of socks, snow boots, a down coat, scarf, insulated mittens and a hat were a requirement. We had no vehicle of our own, so a trip to the store two blocks away meant that everything was covered except the tip of my nose, unless I wanted my glasses to fog up. Going to the store was something I enjoyed.

I never had to worry about carrying too much home because the prices were so high that I never bought very much. So I did a lot of shopping but not a lot of buying.

A death in this place caused a whole different set of challenges. Most of the time non-native people who died would be flown back to the lower 48 to be buried near their families. Or if a person wanted to be buried in Bethel, they would be flown to Anchorage and go into the morgue until spring and the ground thawed out. Tom had to assist with the burial of a school teacher who had served there for many years. She had purchased a plot of ground in the cemetery and didn't want to leave her beloved Bethel. It fell to our church to take care of her request. Some of the church ladies and friends prepared her body for burial. The men had the task of digging the hole in frozen ground. This was a very difficult job. When trying to solve this problem, they began by using a backhoe, but the equipment barely scratched the ice-encrusted surface. Eventually they tried a telephone pole auger and succeeded in punching about twenty holes into the permafrost and then were able to scoop out the icy dirt for her grave with the backhoe. Since the permafrost never thaws more than four feet down, even in the summer, she is probably still very well preserved even today. All in all, it was a very interesting episode during our stay.

Television in Bethel was also unique and was enlightening as to the culture we were in. The call letters for the station were KYUK and the programming lived up to its name. Much of it was reruns and local programming. The local shows were very informative when you could understand the announcer, but the native dialect caused even English to take on a rather raspy, guttural tone. We relied heavily on videos, board games and radio for our entertainment. The local radio station was located in the church and the programming was very good. Tom even learned how to be a disc jockey during our time there and helped with the station.

Going to work and church were events to look forward to. And a dinner or a party at someone's home were considered special occasions. Friendships came easily because everybody needed each other. We relied on one another and knew that we could depend on our new family.

Our first encounter as we drove down the streets of that barren and frozen town could never have prepared us for the warmth and beauty of this village and its citizens. I learned not to let first impressions deceive me. Sometimes the beauty of a community is not lying on the surface but lies deep in the hearts of its people. God knows what He's doing when He directs our footsteps. Don't be put off by outward appearances. The depth, beauty or purpose of a place or a people may not be evident immediately. Be patient and trust His leading. Serve faithfully and you too will find beauty in a seemingly barren and frozen land.

The Woman with the Frozen Arm

Bethel, Alaska was not what Tom and I had expected when traveling thousands of miles to "The Last Frontier". This formidable state was famous for being a land of extreme variety and beauty. But instead of majestic mountains, we found flat tundra. Instead of towering trees covering the whole area, we discovered one lonely tree in front of the police station. Instead of beautiful ornate, softly floating snowflakes, we experienced fine, stinging snow particles that blew across the landscape with a vengeance. Tom and I had come to this unusual village to serve as Assistant Pastors under his brother Glynn. Although we were disappointed by the aesthetic appearance of our new home, we did find a church and a community of very open, loving and friendly people.

One Wednesday night as we stood around drinking hot chocolate, visiting and laughing after church, one of our members came bursting through the door, frantically calling for Pastor Glynn. As Marcus was leaving the church that evening, he came across a snow-covered form lying in a snow bank along side of the road. Unable to move the person by himself, he came back to the church for help. Pastor Glynn quickly threw on his winter gear and ran out the door after him. They jumped into Marcus' El Camino and headed down the road. Sure enough, about six blocks from the church there lay the crumpled body of a woman. She was dressed in a coat, hat and boots but was partially covered with a snow drift. As was the norm this time of year in Bethel, the temperature was well below zero and the wind was howling. Glynn knelt down beside the poor woman, trying to check for any sign of life. She appeared to be breathing but was in very serious condition. After further examination, Glynn found that the woman felt stiff in certain areas of her body, especially one of her arms. The men hurriedly worked together to lift her into their vehicle in an attempt to rush her to the local hospital. They feared that she had already suffered from extreme exposure and that one of her arms was frozen as it felt hard to the touch.

They raced through the village as swiftly and safely as possible. Finally, after what seemed like an eternity, they arrived at the medical complex. Glynn jumped out of the car at the front door of the hospital to run in and alert the staff to this emergency situation. He breathlessly blurted out, "We found a woman in a snowdrift, she is unconscious and in very serious condition, with a frozen arm." In the meantime, Marcus had pulled around back to the Emergency Room entrance. The rather large garage door opened to allow his vehicle inside to the ambulance parking area. The hospital intercom came to life calling everyone in the vicinity to action. Lights were flashing and personnel were running to assist in the rescue of this poor unfortunate woman.

As Glynn made his way back to the ER area, he saw the orderlies removing the woman from the vehicle. She appeared to have woken up from her frozen state and was quite combative as they assisted her onto a gurney. The nurses surrounded the woman as they escorted her into the treatment room. They were attempting to be very careful of her frozen arm, knowing that a limb impaired this way could be extremely painful. By this time, she was displaying a rather violent and drunken behavior with the people who were trying to help her. As they endeavored to remove her snow-covered coat to replace it with soft, heated blankets, she screamed and fought all the harder.

Finally, the coat came off and the hospital personnel stepped back with stunned gasps to find her frozen arm was actually encased in a rather large cast. When Glynn and Marcus saw the commotion and the prominent white cast, they slowly but steadily blended quietly into the background, making their awkward retreat. Their concern for the woman's welfare had been sincere but now it seemed just a little embarrassing to know that the emergency probably wasn't quite as dire as they had thought. A broken arm didn't really rank as an emergency like a frozen arm. And yet, because of their compassion and call to action, this woman's life WAS spared. In her drunken state, she could have easily frozen to death, had they not rescued her, from that snowdrift-covered ditch. However, in their minds, this was not the time for high fives or a pat on the back. So they left without anyone knowing the identities of the two local champions.

The next day, Glynn and Marcus learned that the hospital had been under a huge strain the night before. Several very serious cases had come through the doors of that hospital and the personnel were feeling stressed, discouraged and drained. The shock of finding a broken rather than frozen arm and the laughter that had erupted after our two heroes departure from the scene, served to lighten a very heavy evening. The comic relief that came out of that incident proved to boost the morale of everyone on staff that evening. One of the doctors even woke his wife at three in the morning, when he arrived home from his shift, to tell her the story. She, in turn, laughingly told her Pastor the next day, not realizing that he had been one of the men involved.

The thoughtfulness and concern of these two men not only saved a woman's life but also restored the confidence, courage and commitment of a group of rather tired and disheartened professionals. Hip, Hip Hooray for Glynn and Marcus and their rescue of the Woman with the Frozen Arm!!

Alaska: Frozen Victory

It was October 30, 1984. Tom and I were moving from Anchorage Alaska to a Tlingit Indian village called Angoon. It was located on Admiralty Island across the strait from Juneau, Alaska's capitol. We were taking all of our belongings in a 13' travel trailer that would sleep four. And we were pulling this little trailer with our hard top jeep CJ5.

We had been in Alaska for about ten months, having spent the winter in Bethel and the spring, summer and fall in Anchorage. Bethel had been hard to handle with its long dark days of -30 degree temperatures and 30mph winds. There were no mountains or trees just lots of snow and blustery weather. It seemed like a frozen wasteland. Anchorage had been a heavenly reprieve with majestic mountains, beautiful rivers and breathtaking scenery. There were a variety of flowers, sparkling sunshine, fresh air, beauty everywhere. And even though we had never been north to interior Alaska, we naively thought we had already experienced the best and worst this great state had to offer. In October, the nights in Anchorage were in the chilly 30's but the days were in the mid 50's. The trip we were to make would take us north about 300 miles to Tok, east and then south through Canada down into Haines Alaska where we would drive our vehicles onto a ferry. From there we would travel over the water for about 17 hours to Juneau then finally to Angoon. Considering the distance from Anchorage to Haines, we gave ourselves two days to make this journey to catch the ferry. Extra time was figured in for a little fishing trip at one of the many streams along the way to hopefully catch a lingering salmon or some rainbow trout.

Our little trailer was loaded with household items, food and drink from the big stores in Anchorage because we knew that prices in the village would be much higher. We set off down the road with happy, light hearts. We were looking forward to this ministry opportunity where we would Pastor a small native church while the missionaries went to raise funds to continue their mission work. The day was sunny and warming up nicely. Winter gear was stored nearby because we had learned to be prepared. The back seat was packed full with our Springer Spaniel, Freckles, lying on top of everything. The highway out of Anchorage was dry and the traffic was light. Our caravan traveled along at a good clip, confident that there were plenty of little towns with whatever we needed along the way, because of all the little dots on the map. We went by Wasilla and then got on the Palmer highway heading north toward Tok. After going through Palmer, we noticed that the jeep and trailer began to sway with the uneven road, filled with frost heaves. Tom had to use both hands to hold us steady. When he wanted food or drink, I had to feed him because he couldn't take either hand off the steering wheel for even a second. We also had to lower our speed from 55mph to about 45mph to travel safely.

It wasn't too long until we realized that we might have to forego the fishing expedition. The road did not improve. We also had to deal with road construction and the further north we went, the colder it got. About halfway between Palmer and Tok, we noticed more snow on the ground and then, the snow was on the road but well plowed. The bad roads and lower speed had taken away our timeline cushion of comfort. We needed to make good time and go as far as we could that night. At about eight that evening, we arrived in Tok where we had planned to stay the night. But with more promised road construction and the delays we had already experienced, we decided to go further that night. When we got out of the jeep to get a bite to eat, we noticed that it was pretty cold outside. Inquiring in the restaurant, we were told that the temperature was -30 degrees. We were shocked, not expecting to run into this extreme cold weather. We ate quickly, filled up with gas and headed for Canada. Sure enough, construction was everywhere and slowed us down again. Finally about midnight, we needed to fill up with gas and to find a hotel to rest.

We drove into Beaver Creek, Canada and found a motel/gas station. We were tempted to fill up and go on but the station was closed until 8am. We drove around back to the "office". A woman stuck her curler-filled head out the door and yelled that #4 was open and to go on in. She would get our payment in the morning when we bought our gas. Exhausted, a little worried and discouraged, we pulled in and unloaded our overnight gear. The room was nowhere near fancy, but it was warm and clean, so we were relieved and fell asleep almost immediately.

We awoke early, packed up and were ready to go at 8am on the dot. We bundled up in our winter gear and snow boots with extra blankets close by. The weather was even colder than the night before. Tom started the jeep so it would warm up some but it didn't seem to be warm when we got in. We wrapped the dog in a blanket, throwing extra blankets over us also as we hit the road. We figured that the jeep would warm up as we traveled. The highway was still rough and we could only go about 40 to 45mph but we had to arrive in Haines by 5pm. How were we going to make it? If we just stopped for gas, at this rate, we would barely get there in time. After traveling for about thirty minutes, we realized that the heater in the jeep was not working. The jeep was beyond cold, it was miserable. The dog was snuggled inside her blanket with only her nose showing. I noticed that my toes, though buried in socks and snow boots, were going numb. The scenery all around us was a piercing, brilliant white with low-lying wisps of ground fog. There were no houses, cars or people to be seen anywhere. We seemed totally alone in this vast, deadly, snow-covered wilderness. It occurred to me that we could possibly freeze to death if the car broke down. It was an unsettling thought and something that I had never considered or believed possible until that moment.

We traveled for another hour thinking that one of those dots on the map was a town where we could get some help. They weren't. They were gas stations with a motel or a restaurant attached. Twice, we pulled over to go inside and get warm and twice Tom went back out into that awful, frigid weather to try various things to thaw out the heater. Our hopes of making the ferry were dashed. Knowing that the next ferry was in three days, we were feeling very alone, a bit hopeless and very vulnerable.

As we climbed back in the jeep and started down the road, Tom suggested that we pray together. I had been praying silently all along but this was better. Tom led us in a simple but fervent prayer and then suggested that we sing "Victory in Jesus". Now this was truly a moment of faith, since neither of us felt even one iota of victory in this dire situation. But we did so anyway, stepping out in faith and knowing that the Lord was the only one able to help us.

After several more miles and not too long after our prayer together, Tom had a brilliant idea. He pulled over at yet another gas station/restaurant and broke into our little travel trailer. He had to break in because the door was frozen shut. Then he found our Coleman propane heater, lit it and set it under the dashboard in front of me. At least we would be warm. This was such a blessing. We were able to take off the blankets, scarfs and hats. The jeep was warm. We wouldn't freeze to death. And then a few miles down the road another miracle happened, the car heater thawed out and started working again. Hallelujah, we were going to be late but we would travel in comfort. It wasn't too much longer until another wonder came about when the road leveled out and instead of going 40mph, we were able to go 55 and 60 on dry, smooth roads. We were flying along, confident in the fact that the angel of the Lord indeed surrounded us and had delivered us.

The miles seemed to wiz by. The landscape was still a desolate, brilliant white but no longer seemed so intimidating. The ground fog of misty snow particles had lifted and the sun beamed down on us. The tall snow-covered mountains stood majestically against a pure blue sky. Everything looked different now. God's intervention and His still small voice in Tom's ear, along with our steps of faith, had changed everything.

Miraculously, we pulled into Haines Alaska with two hours to spare. In this lovely little town, the snow was gone and the weather was 50 degrees, clear and beautiful. We took time to stop at a small café to eat and had one of the most scrumptious hamburgers I've ever had in my life. Needless to say, we made it onto the ferry in plenty of time.

Our God is truly an awesome God. One who can take an impossible, dangerous, seemingly hopeless situation and turn it into a victorious song of praise. God is not controlled by the laws of nature. He is not hampered or surprised by any of our problems. He is not thwarted by circumstances. They are just opportunities for Him to show His power, glory and love. When we choose to believe what we already know, then we can step out in faith and triumph before we even see the evidence of that victory. To God be all of the glory. Amen!!

The Tlinget Payback

In the fall of 1984, our time of ministry in Angoon Alaska began. What a beautiful place we had come to, with tall stately trees, lush leafy undergrowth, sparkling bays and waterways. The old church where we had come to pastor was right on the beach overlooking Chatham Strait. The two story parsonage was attached to the little white church. We were to find out, in the spring, that the windows of our house gave us amazing views of God's creation. We would watch hundreds of eagles fishing for herring and then later we would view humpback and killer whales as they traveled through those waters to find their seasonal homes. And many times over the 18 months that we lived there, we witnessed breath-taking sunsets, filmy fogbanks rolling in off the water, violent tides that crashed and rumbled against the pilings under our home and then serene mornings when the water was calm and as smooth as glass. This was a truly incredible place to be, in more ways than one. The scenery was awe-inspiring, the people were a little shy but very loving and kind, and the culture was quite unique and interesting. Soon after our arrival, we would begin our cultural training and would become well acquainted with the Tlingit people and their proud heritage.

When we arrived, it was early November. It wasn't too cold. In fact, it was warmer than Anchorage where we had just moved from. There was no snow on the ground and people were still walking around without jackets. After a twelve hour ferry ride from Juneau, we had pulled into town late one evening. We were in our little hard-top jeep pulling a 13' travel trailer filled with all of our household items. We had known that life in the village would prove to be a little more expensive, so we had purchased and packed food and drinks before leaving the large city of Anchorage. Little did we know that we would be traveling through 30 below temperatures in interior Alaska on our way to this quaint little village. When we started unpacking all of our belongings, we discovered that our three cases of canned colas had burst and spilled out onto the floor of the trailer. What a mess! But we got it cleaned up, salvaging several cans that had survived the extreme cold.

We visited the local general store and found, as we expected, that prices were considerably higher. We had also been informed that there were more reasonable rates at the stores in Sitka Alaska, which was only a five-hour ferry ride away. That is one-way, of course. But for now, we decided that we would look into that particular shopping adventure at a later date.

We had been informed, three days after our arrival, that on the following Saturday, there would be a Tlingit payback party at the large meeting hall, down the road. It was very important for us to attend, so that we could become acquainted with the people and begin learning their customs. We were quite excited and anxious to go to this event. One of our deacons mentioned that the party was to begin about 3pm. At 2:45 on the day of the party, Tom was nervously pacing the floor as I finished getting ready. Even though it was only a five minute walk to the hall, he was afraid that we would be late and tardiness was not an option at our first big event.

We headed out the door a short time later and made it to the hall with a few minutes to spare. As we walked in, we were a little confused and uncertain that we were in the right place. There were no people milling about and yet we could tell that there had been extensive preparation. Dozens of tables and chairs were set up with a large assortment of food items and canned drinks laid out. We stood there looking around, not sure of what we should do, when a couple of ladies came through a door carrying supplies. They looked our way and smiled then continued on with their work. As we watched, a few more people came in setting up sound equipment and microphones. We finally decided to ask someone about the situation.

Tom spoke with one of the men and was informed that 'we were indeed in the right place'. Then he took us over to a table near the front of the hall and instructed us to sit there. As we sat down, we were able to look at everything that had been placed on the tables. Each place setting had three cans of soda, a variety of candy bars, crackers and nuts. There were even other small items that might be considered party favors. After waiting and watching the activity around us, we decided that these items must be meant for us, so it would be okay to drink a cola while we waited.

We sat at this table, watching as the busy preparation increased. About five o'clock, people actually began to arrive for the party, seating themselves and visiting quietly. By six, the hall was quite full, but no one joined us at our table, although each person who came by nodded and smiled our way. Shortly after six, the activities began. There was a head table with many of the elders seated there. The meal was served and then people started going to the microphone to express their gratitude for the help of their neighbors during a trying and difficult time. Some people shared stories about a kindness shown to them. Others told humorous stories about the person who had passed away. It was all very respectful and interesting but we were still a bit confused about what was happening.

There were gifts given to certain people, such as blankets, special dishes and money also. In fact, at one point, WE were given a beautiful ornately painted tin bowl and some dish towels. I accepted gratefully but didn't know why they were given. Prayers were said, songs were sung and more people talked.

After several hours, as the evening came to a close, a woman came by encouraging us to take the extra food from all of the empty place settings around us. This seemed odd to us and when we didn't do as we were told, a man came to our table and informed us that we should gather up the food that had not been used. We nodded and smiled at him and then talked it over after he left. We decided that we would take a few things, but didn't feel like we should gather it all. We noticed that the man watched us and was frowning. After a while, he came back to our table carrying a box. He rather abruptly set it down and told Tom quite sternly that we should fill the box with everything on the table. We looked at each other and then told him that we would do as he said, even though we didn't understand. The man then smiled and shook our hands and left. He did keep an eye on us for a while, but nodded kindly when he saw that we were loading everything into the box.

We discovered later on, that it is a rather important tradition in the Tlingit culture that they share with their neighbors. At a payback party, nothing is supposed to be left behind. Even when you go to dinner at a neighbor or friends' house, they will always offer to send food home with you. Later on when we served hot chocolate and snacks after church, people would take the left over packets of chocolate and cookies home with them. And when we went Christmas caroling on Christmas eve, wherever we sang, we would be encouraged to come in for food and drink. Then goodies or money would be given to take with us as we made our caroling rounds.

We learned that the Tlingit people are very generous and thoughtful, not only with their families but also with newcomers. And even though they were shy and held back their friendship for a little while, once they knew us, we were a part of them forever and held in high esteem. We also discovered that they love one another and love their Lord and Savior Jesus Christ. Sure, they have their problems and differences from time to time, but they always come together during emergencies and pitch in if someone is in need.

The Tlingit people are a beautiful group of people to know and live among and I'm so proud that I had that opportunity. In fact, during our time in Angoon, I was adopted into the Raven clan and given the name 'Kanaseidee'. Even though that was many years ago, I am proud to say that they are among my friends to this day. The consideration, respect, closeness and love of family was definitely displayed between the people of Angoon during their payback parties. And Tom and I were honored to share in their lives and traditions.

Storms Come to Pass (A thanksgiving tale)

It was almost Thanksgiving in 1984. We had moved to the Tlinget Indian village of Angoon Alaska, earlier that month from Anchorage. Our trip to this beautiful little town had been full of adventure and answered prayer, but now we had unloaded, unpacked and were settled into our new home. Life in Angoon was proving to be a very different way of life for us. No longer were we a part of the hustle and bustle of the large city of Anchorage and neither did we have to be slowed down by traffic lights and school buses. Life here, seemed to run at a steady, even pace. There were no stop lights but we did have a few stop signs. It was actually easier to walk to many areas in town rather than go start up our vehicle. But we did use the jeep when we wanted to go up the hill to a friend's home, to the over-priced grocery store or to the senior center. And we needed a vehicle to go to the boat harbor or out to the ferry terminal. But if our destination was along the waterfront, we would walk.

The church was right on the beach, overlooking Chatham Straight. It was an unusual building, being three stories tall. The second floor opened out onto Front Street and this was where the main doors to the church were located. Also a short distance down the walkway was the entrance to the parsonage, which was attached to the church. When you came into the church, you could turn to the left and go down a flight of stairs to the basement, which ran the entire width and length of the building. This was where we held Sunday School and our fellowship dinners and other events. Also when coming into the sanctuary, if you walked several yards to the right, you would encounter the inside door to the parsonage. That door into our home led into the kitchen with a bathroom off to the left and after going through the kitchen you would arrive at the living room. Right before the living room was a rather narrow staircase going up to the third floor where there were three bedrooms. Our bedroom faced west over an incredibly beautiful expanse of water. We witnessed many breathtaking sunsets and other sights from that elevated window over the next year and a half.

The church was built on a hill that sloped sharply down to the seashore. We were able to go out a door from the basement and down a small flight of steps and be right on that beach. There were wooden pilings under the church, that we were to learn later, went quite deep into the ground. It seemed strange for the building to be up so high off the beach because the tide never really got too close, or so it seemed. But we soon learned that the water levels in that part of the world were quite diverse. At one point during the day the water would be several hundred yards out and then later it would only be a hundred yards out. We were informed that the tide could fluctuate twenty to thirty feet depending on the time of day or month. We were soon to learn all of this first hand.

Our first few weeks in Angoon had been full of different activities. Of course, we had church services and were able to become acquainted with the people that way. We quickly learned what the phrase "Indian time" meant. Church began at seven in the evening and at that time we would only have a handful of folks. But by eight o'clock the building would be full of people who loved the Lord and showed it. Their worship, instrument playing, hand clapping and singing were filled with passion for their Savior. Church services were always a delight and something we all looked forward to. And then afterward, we would all stay to fellowship and visit.

Early on, Tom and I were introduced to the Senior Center. We started attending once a week to eat and visit with some of the elders. We loved these moments with them. Sometimes Tom would teach or share a word with them and I would sing a few songs. On other occasions, we would listen as someone else taught. But we always enjoyed our time of visitation. Such a wealth of wisdom and knowledge we found during these talks. After a few months, I was able to acquire a Tlinget song book with the hymns written in their native tongue. With the help of some of my new friends, Beth Jack and Clarice Frank, I was able to learn one of their songs called "At The Cross". I had one gentleman, by the name of Cy Peck, come right up to me to see if I was really singing in his native tongue. When he saw that I was, tears rolled down his elderly, creased cheeks. He was so happy to hear a hymn in Tlinget being sung by a young person. And I was so glad that I had gone to the trouble to learn it, even if it would have been just for him.

Also during our first few weeks, we attended a payback party. This is where the tribe who has been blessed by the support, help and funds of the other tribe, say thank you and give gifts to show their appreciation. This is usually done when there is a death or major incident to the village. Everyone joins together to help, trying to ease the grief by acts of kindness or gifts. This seemed like a great way to show support for each other and bring unity among the people.

We also became familiar with communication within the village by CB radio. We found out that everyone in town had one, but not everyone had a telephone. So a lot of visiting and even business would take place on the CB. Everyone had their own "secret" channel that they used. But if you were nosey and just had to know what was going on, it wouldn't take you long to dial through the forty channels that were available to find their "secret" channel and listen in. Also, unfortunately, every now and then, certain people would have an argument over these airways. That's usually when ours would be turned off or turned down for a while. In fact, the CB radio is how I found out that my Tom had run out of gas while out fishing in our nineteen foot boat and was being towed back to the boat harbor by one of our neighbors. It really wasn't his fault, because the gas gauge had malfunctioned. But much to Tom's embarrassment, the rest of the town was also made aware of this incident because of the CB radio, and many turned out to watch the sight as "the new preacher" in town was rescued and brought home to safety.

Life took on a steady routine with all of these activities and others besides. We had been invited to the home of Peter and Ethel Jack for Thanksgiving dinner. Peter was one of the deacons, and had made it his business to make us feel welcome and show his support for the new preacher. Many of his family were at the special dinner that day and we enjoyed a wonderful time of fellowship and good food. One of the topics of conversation and focus of our prayer together, centered on an upcoming storm, which was due to arrive early the next morning. There were rumors of high winds and waves. And to top it off, a high tide was due during the same time frame.

After the dinner, we all set out to secure anything that might blow away. The men made a special trip down to the boat harbor to make sure that their boats were securely tied down and ready for the storm. Many of the families in this little town earned their living fishing from these boats, so it was very important that every precaution was taken.

Sure enough, early the next morning the rain began to come down in heavy sheets beating against our tin roof. And then the winds began to howl causing the rain to blow horizontally across the landscape. We stayed close to home but became a little concerned when this three story structure seemed to sway a little in the blustery weather. But since the movement was slight, we decided to ride out the storm. As we watched the deluge out of our living room and bedroom windows, we noticed that the tide was indeed higher this time. The angry waves moved closer and closer to our home and church. Surely it would stop advancing up the beach at some point. However, with each new wave it continued its rise over a few hours until finally the waves were crashing into the pilings under the building. There was no beach in sight at all. This was a little disconcerting but not unheard of. That's why the church was securely built with thick wooden pilings, right?

And then we started hearing loud banging noises as with each crashing wave, the entire structure shook. Tom and I went through the church and down to the basement to look out the back door leading out onto the beach. But when we opened the door, the small staircase that had been there was gone and all we could see were those gray raging waters, threatening to come inside the building at some point. We were also able to determine what was causing the loud banging and shaking of the building. The tide had grabbed ahold of some driftwood logs, each about eight to ten feet long. They were being pulled out to sea and then were being thrown against the pilings under the church with each new wave. At that moment, we realized how dangerous this situation had become and ran upstairs to our home to alert the congregation. The CB radio came in very handy that day.

We put out a call to everyone in town to begin praying, briefly explaining what was happening. People of every faith began calling out to our heavenly Father for His intervention and protection. As a precaution, we went ahead and packed up a couple of bags and put them in our jeep just in case we felt the need to leave quickly. We knew that without God's intervention, we would lose most of our belongings to the storm's surge. But within an hour of the urgent call for prayer, the storm began to calm down and the logs floated lifelessly out to sea. The tide began to recede and we all breathed a sigh of relief, giving thanks to the Lord.

Afterward, the men of the church came to survey the structure. The only real damage that had been caused, was to the small staircase that went out the back door, down onto the beach. They inspected under the church and observed where some of the pilings had indeed been hit and gouged by the floating debris, but they were still strong and intact.

That following Sunday, the church was full of believers, who were very thankful to still have a building where they could come together and worship. It was a great day of rejoicing and testimony to God's mercy and protection. Our first Thanksgiving season in this wonderful community was surrounded by much giving of thanks. And we were so grateful for the One who stands nearby during our storms of life.

Storms come to pass, but Jesus comes to stay.

Strange Happenings in the Village

Life in Angoon Alaska was an experience that I shall always remember. For the most part it was a joyful, fulfilling and interesting chapter in our lives. The people in the church and the village were a unique mixture of every class, just like any other small town. People were friendly but a little reserved at first. But once you were accepted into the community, it was forever. One of the unusual aspects of the population was that, everyone native to the area was related somehow. You were either a member of the raven or the eagle clans. It was a wise person who learned how to get along with one and all. If you misspoke or hurt someone's feelings, half the town would be angry with you. And to make matters worse, you would probably hear about it over the CB radio, where all, who tuned in (most everyone in town), would also receive all the juicy details. We didn't personally face this particular trial, but knew of others that did. Fortunately, while we were there, we made many wonderful, life-long friends and didn't seem to alienate anyone.

Being in our early 30's when we came to Angoon, we hadn't dealt with all aspects of ministry and were still a little inexperienced. The preaching, teaching, singing, counseling and fellowship times all went fairly smoothly. We got to know the people and began learning the culture. I was even studying to learn some of their hymns in their native tongue. It seemed to be important to many of the elders in town and it was an interesting and unique language. But one area where we had minimal experience or guidance was in the spiritual darkness realm. Tom and I had rarely dealt with this aspect of ministry.

After being in Angoon for several months, we had some unexplainable things begin to happen. After turning off the television on a rather ordinary mid-week evening, we started going up the staircase to our bedroom. Everything had been locked and secured. Tom waited at the foot of the steps for me to go up to turn on the light in the upper hallway before he turned off the light downstairs. Freckles, our Springer Spaniel always led the way up to our room, when we told her it was time for bed. However, this time when she ran up the stairs, at about two-thirds of the way, she stopped and began to back down again. That was so odd. She didn't turn around and come down, but continued to stare up to the second floor as she slowly backed down to where I stood behind her. I felt the hair on my neck raise and prickle. It was a very strange sensation that sent a shiver down my back. I prayerfully continued up to our bedroom, not seeing anything out of the ordinary. In a few minutes, when Tom came upstairs, so did our little dog. I wondered at what she could have seen?

Later that night, we were all fast asleep, and were jolted awake by the sound of our box fan falling over from where it stood in the corner of the room. At first, I thought that Freckles had knocked it over, but then realized that she was lying on the floor next to me. Tom and I, were suddenly wide awake and sitting upright in the bed. We felt a dark presence in the room and began to pray together in Jesus name. After our prayer time, Tom got up to look over the situation. Nothing appeared out of the ordinary. After a close inspection, he couldn't find a reason for the fan to fall, since it had been propped up in a way to avoid that. I noticed that throughout the whole incident, Freckles didn't leave my side. She stayed put all night long. After a while, we were able to go back to sleep with no more incidents.

A few weeks later, we had a missionary and his young daughter visit us to hold some special services. In our third bedroom upstairs, we had two twin beds and arranged it so they would sleep there while staying with us. After the second night, the missionary told us a strange story. The night before, feeling very uncomfortable and apprehensive, he woke up out of a sound sleep. When he did, he saw an evil spirit hovering over his daughter as she slept in the other twin bed. He immediately rebuked the spirit in Jesus name and it vanished. Fortunately, his young daughter did not wake up. We related our story to him and he also told us of other experiences he had encountered on the mission field. We made the decision to anoint the entire parsonage and church with oil and prayer that very day. After our prayer meeting and anointing session, we never had any more visitations.

Several months later, we had a new librarian in town purchase the house next door to us and move in. She worked tirelessly for over a month, remodeling and updating the little house. We went over and helped with a few things and visited with her some. She was nice enough but wasn't really wanting to associate with the local Pastors in town. She was more interested in socializing and throwing parties in her new residence, where I understand that the wine flowed freely.

After being in the house for only two months, she suddenly quit her job, moved out of her newly renovated home and left town. We wondered about this because she seemed to be liked by most everyone. And also, we knew that she had invested quite a bit of money in the house when she bought it and remodeled it. A few weeks later, she returned to collect and pack the rest of her belongings. We invited her over for tea and she told us what had happened.

Our neighbor began having nightmares after the renovations were completed. She would dream about a Tlinget Indian warrior, painted and in full battle garb. He entered her house, walking through the hallways and to the door of her bedroom. As he began to enter her room, she would wake up and the dream would end. The dream came repeatedly to her, bothering her and interrupting her sleep. On the night that she packed and left town, she had the same dream but this time, when the apparition entered her room, he came and stood over her bed. However, when she woke on that night, he didn't vanish but remained. It was no longer a dream but the visible spirit of that frightening warrior standing above her. We did not hear her screams that night but it did not take long for her to throw on some clothes and leave the house to go to a friends' place for the remainder of the evening. The next day she came back and packed as much as she could before fleeing Angoon. As we visited with her in our little kitchen, she was very insistent that she finish everything at the house before it got dark, so we didn't detain her. We prayed with her and tried to reassure her that the Lord could help her with this, if she would let Him, but she "really didn't want to talk about God". She was determined to get everything packed up and on the Ferry that day. She was well away from the house before the sun set. No one else moved into that lovely little house while we were the Pastors there.

After these various encounters, we had other people in the church share stories about spiritual activities in their town. It was during our time in Angoon when we became vividly aware that there are powers of darkness at work in our world today. Usually they are very subtle so they don't frighten people into taking action. Yes, they are there but we also learned that it is nothing for us to fear. For "Greater is He that is in us, than he that is in the world". We, as God's precious children have power and authority over these things in Jesus name.

Bears in the Final Frontier

When moving to Alaska, we knew that we might come across a bear at some point. The stories about bear sightings were numerous and usually very dramatic. But in our twelve years in Alaska, there were only a handful of incidents where bears were involved.

When Tom went hunting, he was always aware and prepared for a possible bear encounter. In fact, there was a time when he did run across one that caused him to give pause and to proceed very cautiously. As Tom told the story, he was scouting an area near Healy Alaska for a moose hunt on his King Quad four-wheeler. He didn't have his rifle with him that day because hunting season had not yet begun. But he did have his blackhawk colt 45, which was very wise, since that area was known to have bear. In this particular place, his route was on top of an embankment. As he drove up the incline, he came to a curve in the trail. After rounding the corner, the track continued between two steeply elevated areas that resembled walls of dirt and gravel, making the trail go through a forty foot tunnel-like section. After turning the corner, he saw something black run across the path at the other end of the passage. He quickly came to a stop but was committed to the trail, with nowhere to safely turn around. Not sure of what he saw, but thinking it was a black bear, he waited with the engine still purring. Tom felt like he waited about thirty minutes but admitted later that it was only five very long minutes. And then the bear came back up onto the trail. Sure enough, it was a fairly large black bear and it was looking curiously right at my Tom. They continued their staring contest for about ten minutes. Tom sat very still, trying to plan what to do if the bear charged him. He decided that if the animal came toward him, he would put the four-wheeler into high gear and ram the creature, since there was no other way to go but forward. A couple of times the bear turned around and ambled off, down an opening in the path. Then after a few minutes, he returned to the same place on the road to check out his rival. Tom did have his handgun with him but knew that if he hit the bear in the wrong place, it would just make him mad and more dangerous. He really wanted to avoid that scenario. So he decided to wait him out and tried to be patient. Sure enough, after a while, the bear gave a snort and gruffly ran quickly off the trail into the woods. Still Tom didn't move, he wanted to make sure he wasn't just hiding at the end of that tunnel-like route. After another 20 minutes, Tom slowly made his way forward through the danger area and once past it, he took off as quickly as was possibly safe. He came home a little earlier that evening, having had all the excitement he could handle for one day. It felt good to have four sturdy walls surrounding him, listening ears to share his story with, and a hot, home-cooked meal.

Another incident occurred when we moved to the Tlinget Indian Village of Angoon Alaska on Admiralty Island. We were informed that the town held about 600 people and the Island held about 2,000 bear, both black and brown. This concerned me a bit at first, because the ratio of human to bear seemed a little uneven. But once we lived there, it became evident that the bears didn't really desire or appreciate our company, so there weren't too many problems with bear sightings. Occasionally, we would hear about a bear being spotted down at the garbage dump, scrounging for leftovers. Tom and I had only been in Alaska for a little over a year at this point and really wanted to see a bear, so we jumped in our jeep to go get a look. We felt that we were fairly safe in our hard-topped jeep and planned on being very cautious. But by the time we arrived, the bear had run away, possibly scared off by the sound of our engine.

During the time that we lived in Angoon on Admiralty Island, Tom went hunting for deer with some of the men from the church. They took their boat out into Chatham Straight and to a bay located in a different area of the island. After removing all of their gear for the days hunt, the boat was pushed way out into the middle of the bay and the anchor let down so it wouldn't change position. Tom was very curious about this procedure but when he asked why they did this, the only answer given was "You'll see". The three men started their hunt, together sometime and separating other times. Finally after several hours, they were successful in getting a deer. After they cut up and bagged the meat, they headed back to the bay where they had left the boat. Walking back down the trail, they saw their footprints from their trek inland. Not only did they see their footprints but on top of them were the footprints of a rather large bear, probably a grizzly. This was very disconcerting, especially since they were now hauling a large quantity of fresh, bloody meat. Each man became extremely watchful and cautious for the remainder of their hike to the boat. Much to Tom's surprise, the shoreline had receded hundreds of feet from where it had been. The boat that had been anchored in the middle of the bay was now high and dry on rocky ground. They would have to wait for the tide to come back in, before they could make their way through the water to home. So they crossed the rocky ground to the boat, securing all of their gear inside. And since the tide was not due to appear anytime soon, they gathered fire wood and built a nice fire on the rocks near the boat. You can be certain, that none of the men decided on a nap but continued to be acutely vigilant. At least from this vantage point, they could see in all directions and would be alerted early of any bear or other danger. Finally after another hour or so, the tide came in and they made their escape, never actually seeing the huge bear that had followed their trail earlier in the day.

All of my sightings of bear were from a safe environment. One day as Tom and I went on a bus tour through Denali Park, we witnessed what could have been a rather frightening event. The day was perfect, with blue skies and big fluffy white clouds. The temperature was warm when we began the tour but as we ascended the mountain, there was a pleasant but definite nip to the air. Our light jackets were just right for the day. The ride through woods, across streams and down into valleys were all we could have hoped for. We had already seen a wonderful variety of wildlife in the park and were now headed up to a lookout station where we would have a spectacular view of Mt. McKinley. Our bus had been traveling along a road on the side of a mountain, when our driver pulled over onto a special parking area and invited those who wanted to get off to "hike" for a while, to do so. Tom and I decided to stay on the bus this time, but were eagerly leaning out the windows taking pictures and looking for wildlife. As we enjoyed the scenery, we noticed another bus pulled over up ahead, around a couple of curves, a little further down the mountain. Many of their passengers had disembarked and had gone on a short trek down an incline to a small stream. As we watched, we saw the group begin their climb back up to the bus. Unknown to them, there was one small problem, no actually there were two large problems. In between this small band of hikers and their bus were two large, blonde grizzlies. From our vantage point, we could see everything quite clearly. However, because of a small hillside and valley, these folks could not see the bears yet, nor could the bears see them. And it was only a matter of time until the grizzlies would pick up their scent. At that point, we were very relieved that we had decided to stay on our bus even though our group was not in any danger. But we were concerned for the other bus tour group. We were too far away to signal or even yell a warning to them. Knowing that our driver had some sort of communication device, we alerted him to this situation. He used his walkie- talkie and was able to inform the other tour guide, who had accompanied the group, about the danger. The hikers soon turned and began to take a different path up the hill and were able to avoid the encounter with the bears. All turned out okay even though those people had a much longer hike than anticipated, but it was also a much safer hike.

The one other time that I saw a bear was on a trip in my car from Minto Alaska, which is about fifty miles north of Fairbanks. Some of the road is paved, but most of it is gravel, at least it was in the early 90's. On one clear summer evening, as the kids and I were traveling back from a visit with our family in the village, we had a sighting. Actually I was the only one who saw the bear since Judah and Angela had fallen asleep in the back seat. This was a common occurrence since our trips to town always involved a trip of about ninety miles. So after about ten minutes of travel they would both be out like a light. On that particular day, we were traveling at a steady clip down the road. It was a lovely day of bright sunshine and warm breezes. And since I could only travel about 40 mph on the gravel road, I was enjoying a nice breeze blowing in through my open window. Most of the scenery was rolling tundra with a few sparse trees here and there. We came upon a shady, wooded area while coming down a hill, when I saw a large brown bear run across the road in front of us. I was a little startled at first because although we had been in Alaska for about ten years, I hadn't seen a bear this close before. I was very thankful that he was about a hundred yards away and not right on my bumper. I was also thankful that he kept right on going not showing any curiosity in us or our vehicle. He had run out from between a grove of trees, across the road and into another wooded area, not even breaking his stride to notice our car coming down the road. This was a bit unusual since bears don't normally run unless they are chasing something. However, I was glad to see him just the same. But I was really glad that I was able to see him from a distance and not a close up view. A hundred yards away was close enough for this Texas girl.

After the sighting in Denali Park and the one on the road, I decided that I would take precautions when I went out on my four-wheeler around our town. There were numerous trails going to so many wonderful places. These outings became a favorite pastime for the kids and I. Even the ladies of the church would pack a lunch, load up the children and head out on our four-wheelers to the sand pit or gravel pit for a picnic. I didn't usually worry too much about bears when we were all together, because of all the talking, laughing and noise of the engines. But when I went out by myself, I felt that I needed a little insurance, so I decided to carry a distraction for the bear, if I encountered one. I placed a few hot dog wieners into a zip lock baggie and put them inside my fanny pack that I kept close by. I figured that if I saw a bear, I would throw him the wieners and head the other direction while he scarfed them down. Some people have indicated that the wieners would only serve as an appetizer and I would be the main course. My friends were very amused by my action and decided to buy me a bear bell to wear instead. And I dutifully wore my bear bell on some occasions but I also carried my little pouch of hot dogs. Still other friends have teased me about the bear bell as well, saying it was a dinner bell calling the bear to his meal.

However, I never met up with a bear on all of my four-wheeling adventures, so the hot dog distraction theory was never really put to the test. I have, since that time, been teased mercilessly for my reasoning in this situation, siting the fact that I am indeed a blonde. But that's okay, it worked!! RIGHT??

A Dream Come True (at Bonnie Lake)

Summer had come and gone in Anchorage. The long days of nearly constant sunshine, the clear air scented with a vast array of flowers and the busyness of outdoor activities and games had given way to fall. And with fall, came the cooler nights and light jackets, the leaves turned into golden flags waving in the breeze and people excitedly made preparations for the procurement of their yearly meat supply. Our home was no different. Warm clothing was washed and packed, tents and sleeping bags were aired out and rolled up, guns were cleaned and sighted in for accuracy and clean-shaven faces took on a rather rough, scruffy look. That's right, it was hunting season.

There was an air of anticipation as the men purchased a license and tags. Drawings were held designating specific hunting areas to each one. Maps of all sizes and dimensions were laid out and intricate plans were made as the first day of the season drew near. My husband Tom, had been invited to an area called Bonnie Lake.

We had spent a couple of days there, earlier in the summer, so he could spy out the land and get a feel for the area. Fortunately for me, since I'm basically a city girl, there was a very comfortable two story log cabin, facing a lovely little lake. In order to get to the cabin though, we had to load all of our supplies into a small boat to cross over. We could have hiked around the lake but it would have been a long walk with a very heavy load. Needless to say, we were thankful for the boat. The main floor of the cabin had a living area with a couch and comfortable chairs scattered about and a small kitchen with a simple dining table and chairs. A wood burning stove provided the only source of heat. Tom wanted to make sure we were able to burn a few logs and had brought along his axe in case there wasn't wood stored. Fortunately, there was plenty, so he just had to cut some kindling. To reach the upstairs, we had to ascend a ladder-like stairway which led to the loft and the only bedroom. However, this bedroom held a rather unique feature, a round bed. This was not something we expected in the wilds of Alaska, but still, it was nice and very comfortable. It turned out to be a pleasant, little get-a-way for the two of us. We did some hiking and fishing and I enjoyed reading through a good book while Tom did some necessary and extensive scouting.

And now, with summer days behind us, the time had come for the hunt. And this was not just any hunt. It was a moose hunt, something Tom had dreamed of for years. He'd hunted for elk in Colorado and for deer when we lived in Angoon Alaska. He had caught a 30 lb. king salmon and a 100 lb. halibut but never had he gone for game this big. Moose usually range between 800 to 2,000 lbs. My Tom was like a child anticipating his first bike on Christmas morning. He would be hunting with one of his best friends, also named Tom. They would be gone for a few days, up to this summer camping spot at Bonnie Lake, north of Anchorage.

Both men had taken some leave time from their jobs for this special hunt. Of course, in Alaska, employers are very aware of the need for this activity among their employees. All the food, ammunition, special hunting gear and anything else that could be imagined had been packed up and loaded into our friends' vehicle. And with a kiss and a wave they were off on their adventure. Upon arriving at the lake, both Toms realized that they had packed rather heavily because it took two trips in the boat to unload everything. But finally it was all hauled to the cabin and stored away. A nice warm fire was started in the old black stove and a hearty meal of beef stew was prepared. Since there was no electricity in the cabin, lanterns were lit as the sun went down. One of the men would sleep downstairs on the old couch, while the other one would enjoy snuggling into his sleeping bag on that round bed. The fire was stoked up for the night and both men slept well.

Early the next morning when they awoke, they had to build up the fire because it had gotten a bit cold the night before, evidenced by a smattering of snow on the ground. They quickly ate breakfast and mapped out which areas they would scout out, separating for a while and then meeting back up to report what they had seen (this was before cell phones). They were looking for animal signs; poop on the ground, broken branches or foliage and branches partially eaten. Most of the area where they were, was heavily wooded. How moose could maneuver through these woods was hard to comprehend, but somehow they managed. After several hours of walking, looking through binoculars and just waiting for an appearance, they came back together. Had they seen any moose? Yes, but only cows and calves. The licenses they had were for a forked-horn moose, which was a fairly young male without a full rack. They would try again tomorrow. The next day, they decided to stay together, and sure enough they saw moose. But as the day before, none of the ones that they saw were legal for the licenses they had. Toward the end of the day, the two Toms decided to split up again to cover more territory.

My Tom came upon two moose down by a creek. He could clearly see that the one closest to him was a cow, but the one behind her appeared to have a forked-horn or a double tuft of hair, he wasn't sure which. So he took off his glasses and hung them on a tree branch as he looked through his binoculars. He carefully watched the huge animal as it lowered and raised its head several times while it ate. After what seemed like an eternity, he saw it and knew. Yes, it was a forked-horn. His heart began to race as he raised and leveled his 270 to shoot. But then he stopped, remembering something he had read about the size of the antler. Was it legal? Was it too short? He wasn't sure and he didn't want to chance being wrong. He needed to look at his hunting rule book but hadn't brought it with him. He would have to return to the cabin to be certain. If he hurried, he might make it back to this spot before sunset or the moose moved on. He turned to leave and then remembered his glasses hanging on the branch. He would need them to quickly find his way back to the cabin. But they were no longer hanging there. He looked down and found his mangled pair of glasses lying in a fresh pile of moose dung. Not only that, they were ground into the pile as he had accidentally stepped on them. He let out a pitiful groan. Very carefully he picked up the glasses and shook off the rather moist droppings, in hopes of being able to salvage them. They were beyond repair at that point. He knew that this opportunity had been lost. So he slowly headed back to the cabin as the evening sun was beginning to cast long shadows across the landscape. That evening he studied his book, only to learn, that the moose had indeed been legal.

The two Toms got up the next morning full of purpose. They knew the approximate area in which to look. Even before the sun had crossed the horizon, they were on their way back to the site where Tom had seen the moose. Before arriving at the wooded area, they had to cross a large field. As they began their trek across the expanse, they saw two young bulls at the edge of the treeline. The moose saw the men at the same time. Both Toms stopped, enjoying this awesome sight and also trying to determine if these moose were forked-horn. But in the predawn light, there was no way to be certain, so they pulled out the binoculars and watched with amusement.

The moose separated, running in opposite directions. After about 100 yards they both stopped, turned to look at the men, and then looked at each other. Then they slowly walked back together, never venturing too far from the wooded area. Two more times they repeated this game, running in opposite directions, looking at the men then at each other and walking back together. But then as the sun peeked over the horizon, My Tom saw the light glint off the antler of one of the fork-horned bulls. This time, he didn't hesitate, but raised his rifle and fired. Almost before the sound of the shot quit reverberating through the air, the moose was down. The other moose bolted into the woods and both men ran to where Tom's moose lay. Sure enough, he had delivered the kill shot.

As he stood over this moose, tears filled his eyes. He wasn't grieving because he felt bad about bringing down this 900 lb. moose. This kill would provide red meat for both of our families for a whole year. The tears were tears of joy because of an answered prayer. Several years earlier, Tom had been diagnosed with Inflammatory Arthritis, a crippling disease that almost landed him permanently in a wheelchair. He had been told (and at that time believed) that he would never be able to fish, hike, ski or hunt again. He would be confined to hobbling on crutches or in a wheelchair and surviving on pain medicine. But God had given us His assurance that healing was coming and that everything we had lost would be restored. We had seen the healing take place, not long after God revealed His promise through a plain backwoods evangelist. And on this day, after almost ten years, Tom saw the fruit and evidence of that promise completed and his dreams restored. This was an event that would cause the toughest of men to get teary-eyed, and rightly so.

Our Great and Awesome God was and is indeed faithful!!

A Memorable Easter

Easter in Alaska is very similar to the holiday down here in the lower 48. People dress up in new clothes, they have special family outings and dinners. The kids take pictures with the Easter bunny, decorate and hunt for Easter eggs. However, in Alaska, the Easter Egg Hunts are usually held inside since there is usually still snow on the ground. Hiding the eggs in the snow can be fun unless you forget to color them, then it gets a bit tricky☺ And of course, people who honor and love Jesus attend church on that very special celebration Sunday.

This Sunday started out normally. Tom and I were the Children's Pastors of a rather large group of about 125 kids. Muldoon Community Assembly, where we were on staff, averaged about 600 people most Sundays and on Easter the numbers were even higher. The children arrived in their Easter finery, excited about the day. We had prepared special lessons, songs and activities. As expected the numbers were higher than normal but we had anticipated this possibility, so everything was progressing smoothly. About halfway through the service, we heard commotion outside of the Kids Area. Several parents ran into the room, tears streaming down their cheeks, frantically looking for their children. As soon as they found them, they grabbed them up into their arms and ran out the door. Finally, Tom was able to talk to one of the fathers to see what was wrong. He turned to me and said, "There's been a shooting. Stay here with the kids and other teachers. I need to try to help." He rushed out of the room. I stayed there as instructed trying to comfort everyone until all the parents had come for their children.

When Tom arrived at the door of the sanctuary, people were still rushing out, crying and distraught. The room was deathly quiet with only muffled sobs from the few remaining people as they escaped the chaos. As he made his way into the place, he noticed on the right side of the auditorium near the back, that there were two individuals, a man and a woman. The woman was sprawled across the pew unconscious and injured. The man was lying on the floor clearly shot but still breathing, a gun on the ground nearby. The man was writhing in pain and appeared to be reaching toward the gun. Tom pushed the pew back and got down to hold the shooter, while simultaneously pushing the gun out of his reach. Soon, another church member came to help him. Although shot, the man fiercely fought against them, still trying to get to his weapon. After what seemed like an eternity, the police and paramedics arrived and took over for them, restraining the shooter and attending to the wounded.

After speaking to several people and the senior pastor, we found out what had happened that day. The service had started normally with special Easter music, announcements and prayer. The pastor had shared a special story in the middle of the service and had opened the altars for people to come. Many people had gone forward, including the lady in our story. She had been going through a very rough time and she was determined to turn her life around again. She knew that she needed the Lord in order to do this, so she went to the altar and committed her life to Christ. As she came back to her seat, her boyfriend, who had come in the back, came to sit beside her. There was a small commotion as he tried to convince her to leave with him. She refused, excited about her decision for Christ and wanting to hear the Pastors sermon. They argued for a few more minutes and then the man stood up. She thought he was leaving, but He pulled a gun from his pocket, aiming it down at her. She tried to move away but the pew was filled with people, so she was only able to lean away from him. He fired down at her, the bullet going through her jaw area near her eye and out the other side. Miraculously, the person on the other side of her wasn't wounded. When she slumped over and everyone began running, the man turned the gun on himself, aiming up toward his forehead. The bullet only penetrated through the front of his head at an angle. He collapsed but was still conscious and in severe pain.

When the first shot rang out, an undercover officer, across the aisle had pulled his weapon while pushing a mother and child to the floor for protection. But when the man shot himself, the officer holstered his gun and helped usher people out of the sanctuary to safety, not realizing that there was still a threat. (On a humorous note: The woman he had helped protect asked the Pastor later, if he thought that man could have been an angel, because he disappeared shortly after that.)

Both the woman and the man who shot her survived the ordeal. A few days later, the Pastor went to visit the lady in the hospital. As he entered the room her face lit up with a smile and she asked him if he knew what had happened to her. He smiled and told her that he indeed knew what had happened because he was the one ducking behind the pulpit whenever the shots were fired. And she said, "No Pastor, I don't mean that. When you called us down for prayer, I came forward and gave my life to Jesus and then Jesus gave it back to me."

Even though this young woman was shot, she suffered no permanent damage from her injuries. The only difference it made for her physically, was her eyesight. Before the shooting, she had needed to wear glasses. Afterward, they were no longer necessary. Her boyfriend also survived and spent several years in prison. People from the church visited him there and told us that he no longer displayed the violent anger that had plagued him before and eventually he made his own commitment to Christ.

God can definitely take that which Satan means for our harm and can turn it around for our good when we are committed to Jesus.

A most unusual and memorable Easter!

Anderson, Alaska and the Kids

Life in a small Alaskan town is different in many ways than life here in Texas. Summers held wonderfully perfect days of 70 – 80 degree weather with lots of sunshine. One of the few drawbacks about summer in bush Alaska were the mosquitos. The larger cities didn't struggle with the yearly invasion of these pesky critters. But in the village, you learned early on to apply mosquito repellent and then you could thoroughly enjoy the outdoors. They were especially bad out in the woods or while fishing in a stream. In some extreme cases they attacked in swarms where netting was needed for protection. Fortunately, we never experienced that level of infestation.

Another necessity for summer was a watch, because despite your best efforts, it was quite easy to lose track of time. Sometimes, we would still see neighborhood children playing outside at 10pm. In the summer months, the sun came up about four in the morning and went down about midnight. And to be quite honest, it never really got dark. Fireworks at the 4th of July celebrations were not as spectacular as down in the lower 48. It just wasn't dark enough for them to show up well.

Many of our outings as a family or with friends consisted of swimming and picnics. Several families would pack lunches, gas up the four-wheelers and gather up the children. We would ride down a multitude of trails on our ATV's enjoying the beautiful scenery of birch and aspen trees, occasionally pulling over so the kids could pick a handful of the abundant wildflowers. Then we would continue on until we arrived at our favorite picnic area called 'the sandpit'. It consisted of a small lake with trees around half of it and a sandy beach and rocky ledges around the rest. The water wasn't exactly warm but the kids enjoyed it anyway, especially on those rare days when the temperature reached 90 degrees.

In town, we kept a fairly close eye on the children when they went out to play, but weren't plagued with the same fears for their safety that we have down here. Everyone, in this town of about 600, would look out for each other's family. If there was a concern or if the children were getting into trouble, phone calls would be made. The kids also knew this and in some cases, it cut down on pranks.

The winters held a different set of challenges. The kids would play outside as much as we let them, but their time in below zero weather usually consisted of only about thirty minutes at the most. It was quite an ordeal to dress them warmly for this playtime. Shirts and undershirts, warm pants and long johns, socks, a snowsuit, mittens, boots, a hat and scarf were all required attire. All of this took a good ten minutes to put on. Then they would go out to play. They would build a snowman, construct a fort of the icy particles or have a snowball fight if the powder wasn't too fine and would hold together. Sometimes they could sled down a huge hill of snow that had been deposited in front of the house when the roof had been shoveled off. Before too long, they would come in red-cheeked and panting from the cold and the exertion of trying to maneuver in all of their winter garb. Occasionally, Tom would take the kids for a ride on his snowmobile. They would come through the door stomping their feet and laughing, covered from head to toe in a thick layer of fine powdery snow.

At other times, our winter excursions took us to the indoor, heated swimming pool in Fairbanks. This was an outing that we all enjoyed. And since the city was 90 miles away, we would make a full day of it, eating out, running errands and buying groceries. While inside the grocery store, we would plug our three engine heaters into an electrical outlet located in front of each parking space. This helped our car to start again, when we were in the mall or the store for an extended period. Many times, the ride home held the beautiful experience of viewing the aurora borealis. The green, pink and yellow waves of dancing and crackling lights would bring many ooohs and aaahs from everyone.

On one such outing to town, when Tom and I had gone by ourselves, the lights were so spectacular that we pulled over to the side of the road while we were on top of a mountain. We cranked up the car heater to high since it was -20 degrees outside and then we opened our sunroof. What a lovely time we had together, sitting there, holding hands as we watched God's awe-inspiring light display as it danced across the northern sky.

The entrance of the children into our lives came about while we were pastors at a small church in Anderson, Alaska. What a wonderful blessing they were to us. Tom and I had wanted to have our own kids for many years, but never seemed to be able to do so.

When their dad approached us in March of 1990 and asked us to care for Judah and Angela while he went to work, we were thrilled. We had already grown to love them and their two older sisters Kelly and Jean. Dad and the four kids had moved to town in the fall of the previous year and started attending our little church. When the time came for him to go back to his fish cannery job in Kodiak, he ask us to care for the two young ones while their grandma and grandpa, Josh and Dolores, cared for the two older girls. We were great friends with the entire family and so the plan worked well. These are a few of the stories of our life in Anderson together as a family.

Angela was a very sweet and well behaved little two year old. She played well with her brother and with the other kids in the neighborhood. When she was four, a family moved in across the street from us who also had small children. We got acquainted and became friends with them and then they started attending our church. They had a three year old son named Houston. One day Judah, Angela and their older sister, Kelly went over to their house to play. The day was a typical spring day with cool breezes and lots of sunshine. When the kids came home, they were giggling and whispering. I wondered what was going on but figured that they would share with me eventually. Sure enough, Kelly, smiling and dragging her little sister behind her told me an interesting story. That day, while at the neighbor's house, Kelly had performed a wedding ceremony. My little four year old Angela had married little three year old Houston and they had done it in the neighbor's closet. Seven year old Kelly seemed very proud of herself for her part in the event. Angela and her little friend remained good playmates until Houston moved away a couple of years later. My little daughter was quite heartbroken when he left.

Judah was full of life and laughter. At age four, he would wake up at five in the morning, running down the hall with both arms outstretched yelling 'Goood Morning'!! It took a few weeks for us to get through to him that not everyone was a morning person and that some of us liked to sleep until seven or even eight occasionally, depending on what the day held. We encouraged him to try to go back to sleep if possible, but if he couldn't, he could read books or play quietly on his bed until eight o'clock. Then, he could get up and bless us all with his bright and bubbly, morning personality.

Angela on the other hand enjoyed her bedtime and was quite content to sleep until nine if we let her. Each night we would put the kids to bed and tuck them in. Quite often we read a book to them or put on a Dan and Louie tape for them to listen to after we prayed together. I would usually check on them a couple of times before we went to bed ourselves. One night, when I went in to check on Angela, she was still awake. This was rather rare for her because she DID enjoy her sleep. She was almost four years old at this time. When I went in, I ask her if everything was okay. Her eyes were very wide and glowing. She nodded and smiled and began to tell me about a visitor who had come to see her. Not really knowing what to think about her story and being just a little skeptical, I encouraged her to tell me all about it. She said that a man in a long white glowing robe had come to see her. He had stood by her bed for several minutes. She wasn't scared by this sighting at all. When I asked her what he looked like, she said that He was very tall but all she could see were his feet and the bottom of his 'dress'. Everything above his knees was too bright to look at. I smiled at her and assured her that God had sent His angel to say hello and to check on her. I realized at that moment that she had indeed seen an angel or perhaps the Lord himself. If she had been making up such a story, she would have described his face. She wouldn't have just been able to see his feet. What a special gift the Lord gave to my little girl that day. Occasionally, I will remind my now grown daughter of God's visitation to her that night. To me He was saying,' this is my special child whom I have in the palm of my hand and you can trust me to take care of her'. I would need that special promise from the Lord about four years later when she was snatched out of my life and the bottom fell out of my world.

Judah was all boy. He loved to run and race with his friends. He adored Tom and looked forward to their rides on the four-wheeler and fishing expeditions. He would play outside during the summer for hours, digging in the dirt, playing in the fort, swinging on the swings or riding his bike. One year we bought him a BB gun for his eighth birthday. Tom took him out and taught him how to safely fire it, instructing him to never aim it at a person or an animal. Judah was very careful with it for quite some time. But then, one day when Judah, a little friend and his sister were outside playing, I noticed something was wrong. Angela who was about five at this time came in the house looking rather guilty but didn't say anything as she went to her room. Not too long after she came in, Judah came inside looking for her. He also looked a little sheepish and disappeared into her room. I continued working in the kitchen and after a while heard them both come out. When I turned around they were standing in the kitchen doorway and Judah spoke up, asking me to come outside. The words that came next told me that something monumental had happened to him. As we went out the door, I heard words like, "Mom, I didn't mean to, really I didn't. Charlie and me were just trying to hit the cans. It was just an accident. Really, I did it on accident. Will Papa be mad?" As we came across the yard, I looked hard to see what had happened.

I couldn't see anything catastrophic. Everything looked about the same. In front of me sat my large Chrysler that had been wrecked when someone ran a stop sign and broadsided the back fender. The car was still in pretty good shape except for the mangled rear end plus the fact that it wasn't running good at this time. There it sat as usual. In front of it sat a log with some cans on it. The only thing I noticed out of place was that the front passenger window was down. Now how did that happen? Did Judah get my keys, start the car and roll down the window? And then Judah started again. "I'm really sorry mom. It was an accident. I thought it would just make a little hole." And then it hit me!! The window was NOT rolled down, it was gone. Judah had shot his BB gun at a can and had missed. Instead it hit the window which had shattered into a million pieces, scattering glass all through the interior of the car. I just shook my head and sent him to his room with "Oh Judah, Papa will not be happy". Needless to say, Tom was not pleased and Judah received a good scolding and lost the use of his BB gun for a while. But today when we talk about it, there is much laughter.

And then there was the time when I went through a horrible bout with the flu. I was so sick with severe aches and pains, sneezing and coughing, nausea and headaches. Tom was a trooper, taking care of me and the children. He made sure that 5 year old Judah got off to kindergarten with matching clothes and a good lunch. He would wake up two year old Angela, dress her and feed her breakfast. I would get up later in the morning to watch over Angela while he took care of church business or visitation for a couple of hours. Then I would collapse back into bed exhausted and miserable. After being sick for a few days, our morning routine was interrupted. As usual Tom took care of Judah's needs and sent him off to school. But when he went in to check on Angela, he came back almost immediately. As he opened our bedroom door, he very seriously said, "Sugar, I know that you are really sick, but there's no need for both of us to be sick." This statement brought me fully awake as I got out of bed to follow him down the hall. When we got to the door of Angela's room, a strange and rather disgusting smell assaulted my already stuffed-up nose. When I looked inside her room, I couldn't believe my eyes. Everything within the reach of her darling, little arms was painted brown. The bedding, the spokes on the crib, the wall behind the crib and her precious little chubby and diaperless body was decorated with this new color. It seemed odd to me that she didn't seem to mind the smell or the feel of her artistic endeavor. But I guess we are all immune to our own odors. Tom did NOT enter the room. Just standing out in the hallway and peeking inside was causing him to cover his mouth, making occasional gulping and gagging sounds. He made a valiant effort to control his nausea. (On a side note, here was a man who could kill, skin, gut, bag, haul and process a moose without even blinking an eye and yet he was helplessly gagging at his daughters poop. Oh well, we all have our strengths and weaknesses.) But in his defense, he did offer to bathe Angela while I worked on cleaning the room. But before I gave her to him, he proceeded to run warm, sweetly scented bath water and laid out clean, fresh towels for her. I picked up her poop decorated little body and handed her to him. He lovingly took her from me, holding her out away from himself at arms-length until they reached the bathtub. Then he carefully lowered her into the water with a sigh of relief. I then began the work of stripping the bed, wiping off as much of the excess as I could with the soiled bedding. Then the scrubbing with bleach began until everything was clean and sanitary. By the time I was done, Angela was clean and dressed and had eaten her breakfast. Tom escorted me to the shower so I could clean up and then back to bed. He took care of me for the rest of the day and even finished up all the laundry. For many years, we were very careful about who we told this story to, because Angela would get embarrassed. But now she has two little ones of her own and they have both blessed her with this occurrence more than once in their young lives. Isn't there a saying, 'what goes around, comes around'? JUST SAYING!!

Judah had several friends that he enjoyed playing with. Most of these children attended our church and so they saw one another quite often. At the church we stayed very busy, hosting Vacation Bible Schools, Sunday School and Kids Church, Royal Rangers and Missionettes, dinners and fellowship meetings. There was usually something going on each week, only slowing down during the extreme cold winter months when the temperature dropped to 40 and 50 below zero. Even then, we still tried to meet for a Sunday morning service, even if the only family with a heated garage had to go pick people up who couldn't start their car.

It was during one of these frigid winter Sundays that we had another incident take place. In our church, we had an arctic entry way where everyone would initially enter and then a second door that would open into the church itself. The arctic entry helped to keep the extreme cold out of the main building but that little room itself was still very cold. The door going to the outside was a very thick metal door with a metal push bar. Sometimes the door and push bar would frost over. On this particular day, one of Judah's little friends decided that the frost on the push bar looked rather yummy. He proceeded to stick out his tongue to lick it and before we could stop him, the contact was made and he was firmly stuck. We hastened to tell him to remain very still while one of us went to get some warm water. But before we could finish our sentence, he yanked back and ripped a small piece of his tongue loose. The poor child cried out in pain as his parents rushed to his rescue. A hard but valuable lesson was learned that day. And no other child tried such a feat during the remaining six years that we lived in Alaska. Word does have a tendency of getting around.

On another occasion, when the Royal Rangers were meeting, Judah and his friend Charlie decided to play a rather unusual game. We had recently purchased the Disney movie 'Bambi' and the boys had enjoyed an evening together watching it. We didn't realize the impact that this movie had on these two small six year olds until we witnessed their new game in the church fellowship hall. Judah and Charlie were jumping and running around like deer which we thought was kind of cute, but then they decided to take things a step further. Each boy went to the opposite corners of the room, turned toward each other, snorting and pawing at the ground. Then after staring each other down for a minute or so, they ran at full speed with their heads down. As you may have guessed they butted heads together, trying to imitate the young bucks in the movie. As the boys collided, they fell back onto the ground looking at each other in a rather dazed manner. We all stood frozen for a few seconds not believing our eyes. But before they could attempt to get up and try this again, the mothers in the room intervened with scoldings and warnings. To our knowledge, that part of the game was not repeated and I don't think it would have been since both boys offered no argument. Some things are learned very quickly especially when the lesson involves pain.

Children, what a delight and blessing from the Lord. I had my share of pretty rocks, unique seashells, dandelion bouquets, paper chain necklaces, crayon masterpieces and wet, sticky kisses through the years. And I wouldn't trade any of them for a bag full of diamonds.

And although Tom and I never understood why we weren't able to have children from our own bodies, what a joy and privilege to be entrusted with the care for these special kids. And now, I have the distinct honor and pleasure of being called 'Nana' and enjoying all of these treasures once again from my grandchildren. I'm finding that the second go around is just as precious as the first. Yes, life in interior Alaska held many challenges but it also held many blessings and enjoyment. Most of all, it was during this time in our life that God answered our prayers for a family. He provided our precious children but He also gave us a loving church family that became very dear to us and continues to fill my life with love and support even today.

The Dream Song

In 1993 while pastoring a small but growing church in Anderson Alaska, God gave me a special treat in the form of a dream. It was so vivid and real that I shall never forget it. During that time in my life, I struggled with something that I wouldn't wish on anyone, especially someone who loves to sing and is called by God to do so. Working in a dusty room or catching a bad cold could trigger an attack. But the main culprit to bring on the sickening gasping and wheezing were cats. That's right, I fought Asthma and I fought it hard. I know the horrible agony of not being able to breathe. I know the intense longing just to be able to yawn fully because a yawn helped me to breathe more deeply. I had pills and inhalers in my house and carried them with me wherever I went. So as you can see, this was a huge trial in my life, monumental to me.

Then one night, God gave me 'the dream'. Now this wasn't the first time that God had shown me something in a dream. Quite often down through the years, the Lord has blessed me this way, but I don't usually share this because some people don't understand and look at you rather strangely when you try to explain. But I'm going to take a chance with you, my friends. I believe YOU will understand and be blessed. This was a very special dream, one filled with promises.

I was in heaven, standing on a golden brown, dusty country road. There were fenced, green fields all around me. The sky was a pristine blue. Colorful houses and barns were positioned here and there off in the distance. Beautiful flowers dotted the roadside and the grass sparkled with dew. The air held the sweet fragrance of freshly mown grass. The air itself was vibrant, like it was alive. As I took in all the beauty, I began to sing a new song to the Lord. And as I sang, I began to run down the country road as effortlessly as a young child. I marveled that I could run and sing without gasping for air or even being short of breath. It was so exhilarating and made me feel as though I barely touched the ground. The air was alive and swelled around me as the melody and phrases came out. With each uttered word, I noticed that my notes were multiplied. I sang the one note but as it came from my mouth, it split into several harmonies. I had never heard harmonies like these before. And then each note also triggered an array of beautiful colors that surrounded me. The sky was clear with a golden and blue hue and as I sang all of the colors floated out and filled the entire atmosphere. It was incredibly beautiful to see, to hear and to feel everything at once. Not only did all of this overwhelm me, but the fact that I was running on a dusty road and singing at full voice was miraculous.

It was a promise, a promise of things to come. It was a promise of healing and anointing, a promise of His presence and His freedom. The song itself held such beauty with its haunting, sweet melody and simple words of longing and devotion. "Prepare me, prepare me, prepare me to walk with Thee".

And then suddenly, I was awake with the song still on my lips. I got out of bed and went to the piano in the living room, while the tune was still fresh in my mind. I wrote down the words and the melody and years later the Lord gave me verses to go with that simple chorus. Such a unpretentious song, but for me it was one full of meaning. It was my dream song from the Father of Creation Himself.

Today, I no longer struggle with Asthma. The healing came about gradually over the years. However, I do try to be wise and keep my distance from extended exposure to cats. I even got to the place, where I could go visit my mother in Dallas and not suffer because of her long-haired Persian cat. I don't have to carry meds and inhalers anymore. I no longer gasp for air and wish with all my heart to be able to yawn. I can truly sympathize with someone struggling to take in needed oxygen. I find myself breathing more deeply, in an attempt to help them catch their breath.

I am so thankful that I can breathe normally and more freely now and I give God all of the Glory. 'The Dream Song' was indeed a dream filled with promise, a dream that makes me smile with each remembrance, a dream from my Loving Heavenly Father. May you also, my friends, be blessed with such dreams and promises.

The Unexpected Moose Hunt

It was fall and hunting season was drawing to a close with only a few days remaining. Tom and his friends had already gone for their yearly hunt in the beautiful wilds of Alaska and had brought home a bountiful harvest of moose and caribou. All of the work of skinning, cutting, trimming, packing and processing of the meat had been completed and our freezer was full. Winter could now come, for we were set with our meat supply stored away to be enjoyed steadily over the next year.

The hunting equipment had been gathered and readied for storage. The guns had been cleaned, oiled and packed away in cases. The left-over food stuffs had been put back on the pantry shelves. And the four-wheelers had been washed and refueled for another possible activity. When visiting with friends from our community, smiles were numerous and sighs of relief could be heard, as they sat together relating hunting stories from various adventures. A few of the town's people were still frantically pursuing their game, but for the majority of the people, their season had ended. Now was the opportunity to put the feet up, pull out all of the pictures and relive the thrill of victory and the agony of defeat, because there was always a combination of both at this time of year.

Home, at last, with only a few odd jobs to do, Tom was quite content to sit back in his recliner with a big cup of hot chocolate in one hand and the TV remote in the other. Preparation for the winter months was now complete with the attainment of our meat supply. Firewood was cut, stacked and stored. Vehicles were tuned up and outfitted with three different engine heaters. The arctic entryway, coming into the house, was cleaned and filled with every imaginable piece of clothing that might be needed to protect from the impending frigid weather. Caulking and weather stripping had been applied to windows, doors and any cracks to be found. The wood burning stove had been cleaned out and stood ready for its important job of maintaining a comfortable temperature inside our home, while the outside world dipped to a bitter and miserable level. The snow could fly, the temperatures could fall to well below zero, the short dusky days and long dark nights could now make their appearance. Everything was ready for the long, cold winter.

Tom's hunting season was over and he was glad. It had been fun and enjoyable, but as was always the case, it was a lot of hard work and very tiring. A nap was in order. Ahhhh, Zzzzzz.

As Tom settled in for an afternoon of relaxation and laziness, the phone rang. He groaned, not wanting to move. "A pastor's job is never done," he thought. Since this was before caller ID, he reached for the phone, not knowing who was calling and interrupting his much-anticipated nap. It was his brother, Glynn, who he was actually glad to hear from. Glynn always had some good stories to relate and Tom was chomping at the bit to recount some of his own adventures. They were always ready to regale each other with a bigger and better story, each trying to one-up the other. But this brotherly time of sharing tales was not to be. His sibling needed Tom's help with something. Glynn had been contacted by the pilot of a rather well known evangelist. This minister was in Alaska for three days before needing to travel to California to preview the release of a movie about his life. And while he was here, he wanted to go on a one-day moose hunt. The permits and licenses were all in order. Could Tom help? The temptation to just say 'NO' and go back to his siesta was quickly squelched. Tom was very familiar with the evangelist and was honored to be able to arrange this hunt for him, even though it meant another session of preparation, planning and repacking some of his equipment. But this hunt was only for a day, so it wouldn't be as difficult or tiresome to plan and execute. No tents, sleeping bags or cooking supplies were needed. This time they could get away with minimal equipment such as four-wheelers, guns, game bags and lunches. This would be a cinch, right? So it seemed!!

He agreed and laid aside his lazy plans and began preparing for the following day. The recliner would have to wait for another time because NOW there was an array of things to be done. Glynn would fly the evangelist, his grown son and the airplane pilot to our airstrip outside of town where Tom would pick them up before sunrise the next morning. Tom was in charge of loading all necessary equipment and three four-wheelers onto a trailer in preparation for the hunt. They would bring their own personal supplies and weapons. When everyone arrived they would head to a hunting area called 'Ferry' just outside of Healy, Alaska.

Tom was packed and ready to go when he received the call the next morning, but had to drive thirty miles out of the way to the

Nenana airstrip, instead of ours, to pick up the three men. Someone had forgotten to leave the runway lights on at the Anderson airport. However, Tom was prepared with everything he thought they would need, including extra lunches that I had made just in case the other guys had forgotten theirs. They would spend the whole day on the mountain and head back around sunset, hopefully with a mighty moose in tow. I made plans to have a hearty, homemade moose stew and cornbread ready for them when they arrived at our house that evening. And I set about cleaning and straightening in readiness for our special visitors.

The men made it to 'Ferry' just a little before sunrise. After unloading the vehicles and equipment, they headed across the river on the old railroad bridge walkway. In the predawn light they traveled up a broad gravel road leading to an old mining camp and ultimately to a plateau. The trail from the mining road to the plateau was rather narrow and winding. Tom had been this way many times before, so he knew it well. As they approached the final leg of the trail that would climb steeply onto the plateau, he cautioned and instructed everyone to stay close, leaning forward over the handlebars of the four-wheelers to help steady them as they ascended the final, precipitous twenty feet to the top.

Everyone made it to the summit without incident but paused in stunned awe at the glorious view that awaited them. They felt like they were on top of the world. The plateau was shaped like a wide horseshoe and Tom knew the area on the other side would most likely contain moose. The day was beginning to brighten and was beautiful with a panoramic view of majestic, purple mountains off in the distance. The heavens displayed sparkling blue skies and held a crispness to the air, that made you want to just stop and breathe it in deeply. There was no wind, but white clouds with a golden and lavender glow floated languidly high above their heads. The grass and tundra glittered with a fresh coat of sparkling dew as the sun made its way above the horizon. After allowing everyone to take in the spectacular view and inhale the moist air for a few minutes, they started off at a leisurely but steady pace across the vast plateau. It was going to be a glorious day.

After making their way across the wide expanse, they came to an area that overlooked a massive valley. This would provide a good vantage point to scout for moose and plan their course of action. The four men split up into two groups, one group traveling a little farther around the ledge for a different view of the valley. Four-wheelers were parked and turned off. The peace and quiet of the morning resumed and began to lull all creatures in the area into a sense of wellbeing.

Binoculars were whipped out as well as some breakfast sandwiches, granola bars and coffee. In Tom's case, it was a toasty thermos of hot chocolate that he reached for. Communication was kept to a discreet and quiet level, using hand gestures and low voices. The walkie-talkies were used sparingly between the two groups in an effort to maintain the impression of security.

After a time of careful and quiet perusal, the men began to spot movement in the brush and trees of the valley. There was nothing distinct in their sightings, so they decided to ride the four-wheelers down closer to the line of birch trees in two separate areas for a closer look. They were going to hike from there until they spotted some game. Tom and the minister would go one way. The pilot and minister's son would go the other way. If shots were fired, they would all regroup.

After a couple of more hours, in the early afternoon, Tom and his companion heard gunfire. Knowing that this probably meant that a moose was down, they hurried back to their four-wheelers and headed off in the direction of the shots. Sure enough, as they came over the last rise, they saw the minister's son down in the valley with a 1,000 pound moose lying on the ground. But what he was doing was a bit confusing and quite unbelievable. He was dragging the huge animal toward a pile of brush and bushes. This 250 lb. man was actually moving this creature by himself. How was he doing that? Why was he doing that? Was there a problem? As they came closer, they realized that there WAS indeed a problem. The moose that he had shot did not meet the size requirements for that area. It was illegal. He was immediately apologetic, not realizing his mistake until the trigger had been pulled and it was too late. He panicked and was attempting to hide the evidence until a solution could be found. He knew that if he was confronted by a strict, hard-nosed game warden, all weapons, four-wheelers, equipment and even his dad's airplane could be confiscated as a fine and penalty. His dad and Tom also realized the gravity of the situation but stopped him from any further activity. They would just have to deal with the mistake and hope for mercy from the authorities. It was decided to prepare the moose for transport back to town, where the necessary phone calls would be made.

About that time, one of the men from our town, who had also heard the gun shots came upon the scene. He was very concerned about what he saw. Tom, being Mayor of Anderson, at that time, knew the man quite well. He assured him that it would be handled honestly and appropriately. Then everyone began the arduous task of cutting up and bagging the moose meat to haul back to town and turn over to the proper officials. This took most of the rest of the afternoon. But finally, right before sundown, they were loaded onto the four-wheelers and ready to travel back to the jeep and trailer. Tom knew that they had to hurry because once the sun set, it would be next to impossible to find the steep trail descending off the plateau that led to the mining road back to civilization. He took off across the tundra of the plateau at a brisk speed, focused on a mountain peak that indicated the general area of the needed trail.

As he bounced around in an alarming manner, he glanced back to see if everyone was okay. What he saw caused his heart to stop beating for a moment. They weren't behind him! As he turned his vehicle around, he saw the taillights of the other two four-wheelers headed in the wrong direction. He chased after them at a speed that was definitely pushing the boundaries of safety. After catching up with them, Tom directed them back to the general vicinity of the needed trail. However, by this time the sun had set and it was beginning to get dark. The headlights of the four-wheelers were turned on and the men set off, intent on finding the trail.

As they approached the area where the trail should be, the wind began to blow. A chilly breeze caused all of the men to zip up their jackets and reach for the hats and gloves. An unexpected storm was blowing in. Tom began to get a little concerned because they had not brought any supplies for spending the night on the mountain. He had to find that trail! But the thought of going down it in the dark was not a pleasant one. However, he knew that if he could find it, they could make it out. He drove his four-wheeler to the edge of the plateau, trying to shine its lights down to find the path. But the lights just shot out straight ahead not allowing for any illumination downward. That wasn't a problem, for Tom had put new batteries in his large flashlight. He would just walk along the ledge with the light until he found the right trail. As he dug the flashlight out of his backpack, he realized that the bouncing around on the four-wheeler had either turned it on and had run down the new batteries or broken the connection somehow. It was useless. So he went back to the four-wheeler while the other men huddled anxiously nearby. Tom decided that he was fairly certain where the trail was and would drive down first to test his theory. Once the headlights were pointed downward, he would know whether he was right or wrong, but he would also be committed to that path.

As Tom pointed his ATV down the suspected trail, it became abundantly clear that he had made a mistake. He and his machine fell a dozen feet to a ten-foot ledge below. Beneath that was a much steeper and dangerous cliff. Fortunately, he stayed on the vehicle landing away from the edge of the precipice. Very carefully, he turned around and, leaning over the front of the four-wheeler, was able to climb back up the side of the crag to the plateau and safer ground. This gave everyone such a fright that it was decided that they would have to wait until morning's light to try again. In the meantime, the wind had increased and the temperature had decreased. They would all climb down to that ten-foot ledge, which was out of the wind, and spend the night.

Everyone dug in backpacks for anything and everything that would help them to stay warm for the night. The four men lay down on the cold ground, huddling close to one another in order to share their combined body heat. Tom was next to the evangelist on one side and noticed that if he moved away from him in the least, the man would start to shiver violently. He realized that because of severe injuries the minister had endured when he was younger, he was more susceptible to the cold. The man's son and Tom made it their mission to stay as close to him throughout the night as possible.

After a long and miserable night, at the first hint of dawn, Tom was up scouting for the trail. As it turned out, they were only about twenty feet away from it. Everyone got up, eager to be on their way to a heated jeep, hot coffee and ultimately a hot breakfast. The trip back to our house was uneventful and made with grateful hearts that no one had been injured. And although very uncomfortable, no one had suffered from the exposure to the elements.

I was up very early, anxiously watching for this group that should have come home the night before. I hadn't slept very well and used every waking opportunity to pray. The stew from the night before had been put away. I had called a couple of men from the church about the situation and they were prepared to go up to the area if I didn't get word from the hunting party in the morning. When the men arrived, my relieved smile and the smell of coffee greeted them as they came in the front door. No one seemed to mind that it was very strong since it had been brewing for some time as I waited for their arrival. After providing everyone with a hot drink, I quickly whipped up a breakfast of pancakes, eggs, sausage and toast.

As the men ate their breakfast and warmed up even more, the mood was open and friendly, although with an underlying somberness and concern. The evangelist was waiting for the State Offices of Fish and Game to open so he could make his phone call and report the incident. We all prayed together about the situation and trusted the Lord for mercy and favor.

Finally the time arrived and he made the phone call. Everyone was nervously quiet as we listened to his side of the conversation. He spoke in a humble and apologetic manner. It appeared to be going well but it seemed to take much too long. As he hung up the phone, he turned with a smile on his face. They appreciated his honesty; there would be no fine or penalty and we just had to surrender the moose to the game warden in Nenana. They would find a needy family in the area who could use the meat. Everyone breathed a sigh of relief with expressions of praise and thankfulness. God had granted us favor.

This simple one-day hunt had turned into an ordeal that would never be forgotten by anyone involved. In the midst of many dangers, God had been faithful. He had honored our men for their words and deeds of integrity and righteousness. It wasn't until much later, after our company had left and Tom had settled into his recliner for that long anticipated nap, that I found out about the severe danger he had been in and how close to death he had come. But again, the Lord had intervened and protected my husband. This was only one of many incidents where God Almighty had stepped in to help and protect. He is indeed a good Friend to take with you on an unexpected, end of the season moose hunt.

Hunting vs. Roadkill

Life in Alaska was very different and quite unique. In our twelve years there, we lived in four very diverse areas. First there was Bethel, which consisted of six months, December through May, of extreme cold and wind. It had frozen tundra and no mountains, frozen rivers with ice thick enough that a semi-truck could safely use them as a highway to travel from one village to the next. The second place was Anchorage, a big city with all the conveniences. It had majestic mountains, sparkling waterfalls, an overabundance of flowers, streams teaming with fish, wildlife everywhere and beauty beyond compare. The third place was Angoon, a Tlinget Indian village on Admiralty Island down in southeast Alaska. It also held a different kind of beauty with its huge trees, lush undergrowth, juicy berries, incredibly beautiful channels and straits. The land was full of all kinds of wildlife, such as black and brown bear, deer, foxes and wolves. The waterways held seals, dolphins, sharks, humpback and killer whales, shrimp and herring. The sky was filled with many varieties of birds including hundreds of bald eagles, crows and ravens. The fourth area where we lived was interior Alaska, and again it was very different from the other three. Anderson Alaska had birch, evergreen and aspen trees, wildflowers along numerous backwoods trails, streams full of trout and salmon coming home to spawn, moose and caribou, beaver and wolverine, mink and lynx. Although there were no mountains near our town, we could see them off in the distance including the awe- inspiring Mount McKinley. And if desired, we could reach them within an hour.

The last three places held a few things in common that made my husband's heart rate elevate at certain times during the year. They each had superb areas to fish and hunt, and you can be sure that it didn't take Tom long to find all of the best places. I'm sure that Bethel had those areas also but we weren't there long enough to investigate and take advantage of them.

It was usually around July that the hunting fever began. The fishing equipment had been out and had been utilized since some time in May. But now summer was half over. Our 20 hour days of 60 - 80 degree weather were coming to a close. The family picnics, four-wheeler rides to the sand pit to swim, walks through a forest of birch and evergreens, outings to take the kids fishing at the clear stream down the trail from the house and hikes to pick bouquets of wildflowers, were winding down. The garden was overgrown and harvested for the most part. The outdoor chores and projects that had to be done before winter, were mostly completed. Winter was coming. But before winter made its frigid entrance, the season that most of the men in the town looked forward to would arrive. Autumn!! And with autumn came hunting season.

In August the rains began and the leaves began to turn brilliant colors of gold and then fall from the trees. The weather became chilly with shorter days and longer nights. The northern lights became more noticeable, with the increased hours of darkness, as they streaked across the heavens in crackling waves of greens, pinks and yellows. My husband's beard seemed to grow thicker and longer with the anticipation of colder weather and the prospect of camping outside in this beautiful wilderness. Vehicles were serviced, equipment tested, guns cleaned and polished, bullets pressed and loaded, winter gear aired out and mended. Maps were pulled out and meticulously reviewed as discussions were held and plans were made.

The preparations were extensive, spilling over into my everyday life also. Meals were planned, food obtained and packed, keeping in mind the limited space on a four-wheeler. Ice chests were scrubbed and disinfected, the freezer was cleaned out and organized making room for the fresh supply of meat that was sure to come. The meat grinder was scoured and tested, containers set aside and stacked.

Everything was made ready to handle, clean and process our yearly supply of red meat, whether caribou or moose. One or the other, sometimes both, would bless our household and the other households of the people in our church and town. If one family somehow came away from the hunting season without a kill, then the other residents would share their bounty. No one was left out.

The men of the church usually planned their hunting trips together, which provided a safety factor that the wives were very thankful for. And these hunting excursions brought a bond of friendship and unity that were invaluable. And while the men were gone on their quest, the ladies would also travel to Fairbanks, 90 miles away, on their own hunting trip for bargains and sales. We would take the kids to the indoor, heated swimming pool and out to eat at local restaurants. We would walk the local mall and spend time in the small arcade, playing games and being silly. The kids hard-earned summer chore money burned a hole in their pockets, so we would then plan on a couple of hours in Woolworths dime store to let them spend it. Then we would take time to buy a coke float or chocolate sundae at the old time soda fountain in the store. It was a time of much laughter and fun. While the men played, so did we. We knew that once that trigger was pulled, playtime was over and the real work began for them and for us. But that was okay, because our families would be blessed for almost a year with nutritious food from this activity.

As the opening day of hunting season approached, the excitement was tangible. The hunting trips were the main topic of discussion wherever you went. And as you can tell, weeks of preparation had been going on. And even with all of the hard work, the energy level was high and the adrenaline was pumping. No one felt tired or weary but were possessed with anticipation.

The hunting consisted of a few days at a time, each week for about a month, which was usually the length of the season. Of course it all depended on the permits and tags each man was able to acquire. Some went for moose, others for caribou, and then again some hunted for dall sheep or bear. Tom at one point or another hunted for all of these except bear. He never specifically went looking for a bear but if he had encountered one that threatened him, he was prepared to shoot.

There are many hunting stories that could be told here but those need to be saved for another time. The main point here is that hunting season was greatly anticipated with much excitement and preparation. And every year, after all of the work of the hunt, hauling the animals, curing the meat, grinding and cutting, packaging and storing, unpacking the gear and putting it away till the next time, we would sit back relieved to have it over but satisfied and thankful to have a full freezer.

And then a month or so down the road, after the temperature had dropped consistently below zero and the ground was covered with snow, we would get a phone call from the state troopers. A moose had been hit by a train or a car and was at a certain location along the highway. Did we want the meat for some of the families in our community? Our church was on the call list for handling ROADKILL.

Now in Texas, if someone mentions roadkill, the image that comes to mind is a raccoon, opossum, armadillo or even a skunk. Not really something a person wants to scoop up off the road and take home for dinner. But in Alaska, roadkill usually meant a 1,000 lb. moose, give or take a few hundred pounds.

Moose were very curious creatures. For some reason, they thought they were invincible and would amble calmly along the highway, jumping over snow berms and stepping into traffic if they felt the urge. There were many times, when we lived in Anchorage, that we would see them traveling through peoples yards and then lope off down the neighborhood street as though they were right at home. In town, they didn't really have any need to fear vehicles because people were very aware of them and cautious around the moose. But out on the highways, it was another story. Sometimes the moose would appear suddenly before a car could swerve to avoid them. In those cases, the results of the collision were not pleasant for either party. But the calls that we usually received for roadkill, had to do with a moose encountering a train. In that instance, the moose was always the loser. Somehow, word of this danger never seemed to get out to the moose population. There were no 'moose vs. train 101' classes being taught to their young to warn them of this. Moose had the strange notion that they could take on a train. It has been reported that they were known to put their head down and charge a train that was invading their territory with its loud whistle and obnoxious headlight. And the outcome was always the same, one very dead moose. Sometimes, the moose would try to get out of the way, but wouldn't make it totally off the track in time. In that case, there would still be a good amount of meat to be had, from one of these incidents. But if the moose was one of the ones that bravely yet unwisely challenged the train, there wasn't usually much salvageable meat left. Moose hanging out on a train track was a fairly common scenario in Alaska, so the trains were equipped with a device to pick up the moose and deliver it to the next main highway for retrieval, so that the meat wasn't wasted.

What is interesting about all of this, was our reaction when we received these phone calls. We were glad to get the call because we knew that someone in the community needed the meat but at the same time, we dreaded the call. It just didn't hold the same amount of excitement that the hunt held. Yes, the pickup was more convenient, since we could drive a truck or jeep right up to it, However, it was much colder now and dealing with frozen meat was not a pleasant prospect. We needed to act quickly. So Tom would get help from one of the men in the church, even if the call came in the middle of the night. The next morning, I would begin making phone calls to find someone in town who was in need. Usually, the people were thrilled and would help with every step of the process of obtaining the meat. Also, they would clean, prepare and package their own meat. So we were off the hook there.

You would think that we would look forward to those phone calls, and some of the time we did. But it just didn't hold the same level of appeal as the 'mighty hunt'. Tom and I discussed it numerous times, wondering at ourselves and our attitudes. What a blessing it truly was, but somehow we wanted all of the work and preparation of the hunt. Aren't we fickle people? Oh well, either way, God continued to bless us exceedingly and always provided a bountiful harvest, whether by roadkill or through the 'mighty' hunting expedition. Thank You Lord!!

Finding God in the Pain

In January of 1996, Tom and I moved back home to South Texas from the great land of Alaska. We had spent twelve years of our lives there in ministry. We had experienced life to the fullest, doing things we never could have planned and walking down paths of service that we never could have imagined. God had blessed us abundantly above all we could have ever asked or thought possible.

One of our greatest blessings while there, were the children that the Lord brought into our life in 1990. Judah, Angela, Kelly and Jean became the very center of our existence, along with the Lord of course. We had been unable to have children of our own, so when the children's father approached us about keeping them while he went to work, we were thrilled. The older girls moved in with their grandparents, who were and still are dear friends of ours. Judah and Angela came into our home and hearts. Angela was 22 months and Judah was almost five years old. The arrangement, at first, was to be for six months while their dad was working at a fish cannery in Kodiak, Alaska, a few hundred miles away. The six months stretched, happily for us, into 5 ½ years. We loved these children dearly and became one big happy family. Both families, with the older two girls and the two younger children, did everything together. When dad was home from his job at the cannery, he would visit the kids or have them come stay the night at his house in town. The situation seemed to work, even though it did have its tense and challenging moments.

However, in 1995, something changed. The dad came home from his job, in the fall as usual. But this time, he insisted that his children leave our homes and move back in to his house with him. The reasoning behind this decision was never really understood, but the result of it was devastating to us and to the kids. Although the children loved their dad dearly and part of them was glad to be home with him again, another part was grieving intensely for the families they had been raised by and shared life with for more than five years. Their security and stability was severely shaken. We did what we could to help them through the changes that came about because of these circumstances. But we weren't able to provide answers because we didn't really understand it ourselves. To be quite honest, we were hurt, angry, sad and grieving over the loss of our family. We felt utterly helpless to find solutions and to deal with this intense level of pain. Almost every day there were phone calls from teachers, friends and the children themselves, asking for our intervention and help. Angela was in 2nd grade, at this time, but was unable to focus on her work. Teachers would call me to come to the school to just sit with her so she could function. She was happy to be with daddy but was severely depressed by not being with us. I would go to the school sometimes to help fill the void and to help her deal with the changes in her life. But then, when I took her back to daddy's house, I would go home or to the church and weep uncontrollably. And I found out years later that she cried herself to sleep almost every night. It was pure torture to love them so deeply and to be forced to leave them in a less than ideal situation. Judah was ten and also missed us greatly but he needed his daddy's approval and love, so he adjusted a little easier to the changes. He basically buried his grief by watching lots of television and playing video games.

During this time, we sought God through scripture and much prayer. One of the passages that the Lord gave to us was Jeremiah 29:11. "I know the plans I have for you", says the Lord. "Plans for good and not for evil, plans to give you a hope and a future." I remember praying at the church, one winter day, crying out to the Lord for help and direction in all that we were facing. I poured out my heart telling him how much I loved these children and how helpless I felt. He spoke to my heart, "Let go of them, give them to me." I resisted strongly at first. How could this be? "But I love them and I'm supposed to take care of them," I answered. He said, "I love them more and if you will release them to me, I will look after them for you. Do you trust me to do this?" He was telling me to take my hands off of the situation and to let Him take care of it. So after some more debating, I spoke the words out loud, "Lord, I know that I can trust you with my children. I know that You love them more than I can imagine, so I give them to you. Please take care of them for me. They are yours."

Not many days after that prayer and those words of commitment, we decided that God was directing us to resign the church, leave the kids in Alaska with their dad and come home to South Texas. Leaving our children behind while we moved thousands of miles away was the most devastating thing we had ever done. We left not knowing if we would ever see them again. In our minds, it was a loss much like death. Their future and ours was totally in God's hands.

I believed that God had a plan but at the same time I was dealing with the acute pain of separation. My precious children were gone from my life. There was a huge, gaping, raw wound that I could barely endure. I couldn't shop at Walmart or the grocery store sometimes because I would see mothers with their own kids and break down crying. At family get-togethers, where nieces and nephews were running around, I would have to leave the room for a while because of the intense grief I felt. This feeling of loss continued for about three months.

After being gone from Alaska for a while, we traveled to Kansas to visit my dad and second mom. It was a good visit but I was still under this cloud of debilitating grief. At one point while we were there, I went to lay down in the bedroom for a nap. It was then that I prayed for God to take me home to heaven. I just couldn't bear the pain. The wounds from the loss were still so fresh that I didn't think that I could deal with it anymore. While I was laying there begging God to just let me die, not thinking how this request would affect anyone else, I felt a sharp stab in my head and severe discomfort in my throat. This was pain I had never had before, in places that had never hurt before. And then I heard His voice. "Child, I can arrange for you to come home, if that's what you really want. Is it?" It startled me to realize what I had really been asking for. I told Him, "No Lord, I don't really want to die. I just don't want to hurt like this anymore!" Once more, on that day, I gave the children to the Lord. The rest of our visit, although not pain free, went better after that. I was able to enjoy our time with my parents, playing games and even laughing. The situation had not changed, I had. Don't get me wrong, I still missed the children and I still hurt but they were securely in God's hands now. And I learned that I could trust Him to take care of it.

About a month later, we got a phone call from their father. He wanted to know if we wanted the kids to come down and live with us in South Texas. He had to go back to work at the fish cannery and "that was no place for children". He had asked them who they would like to stay with and they had told him that they wanted to come back to us. Did we want them back? "DID WE WANT THEM BACK??" In our eyes the question was ludicrous but we understood that it was his way of correcting the situation and doing what was best for the kids. And it was a question that we could answer joyfully and assuredly. YES!! YES!! YES!!

We told him that we would make arrangements to fly up to Alaska, as soon as possible, to get them. He informed us that he was driving down in a couple of weeks and that we could meet them in Missouri. Sure enough, two weeks later, they were back in our arms, lives and care once again. And there they remained until each one was grown, married and began a family of their own. And now, because of God's faithfulness, favor and intervention, I am privileged to be called 'Nana' by seven beautiful grandchildren.

God had been true to his Word. When we released them into His capable hands, He was able to work out all of the dynamics of what needed to happen. And when I gave Him my pain and hopelessness, He was able to provide for my healing and restoration.

Reflections of a Widow

The Memorial Service October 11, 2013

My Tom and I, forty years together. In some ways it seems so long and in other ways so short. Oh, the adventures we've had together, the sights we've seen and the people we've met. It all began in Waxahachie Texas at Southwestern Bible College.

I met Tom in the spring and became friends in the fall. We connected because of the death of a mutual friend over the summer. We would meet for breakfast and walk to classes together, at first talking about our friend. But then we started talking about everything. Tom went to school in the morning and would head for work about 2pm. He didn't get home from work until after my 11pm curfew, so in order for us to talk together, he would come stand beneath my second floor window in the dorm and throw pebbles to hit the glass. I would open the window and we would talk for a while. After a week, I got the bright idea to hang a string out the window with a small bell attached inside my room. You must understand that in those days curfew was strictly upheld and there were no phones in the dorm rooms. That's right, we actually survived without cell phones.

People began to tease us about having a 'relationship'. We just smiled and said "We're just good friends". One day, I was unable to meet Tom for breakfast and didn't show up for classes. He tracked down my roommates and found out that I was sick with strep throat. I was able to briefly come down to the lobby to see him, and when I did, he prayed for me. Such a simple but powerful prayer it was, and when he was finished my throat no longer hurt. I remember repeatedly swallowing because I was so amazed that such a simple prayer had brought me such immediate relief. I learned that night, that Tom was a sincerely caring and faith-filled person that I could trust and count on.

As the weeks went by, we realized that our feelings for one another went deeper than a friendship. Yes, we were friends but there was a depth of love there that began to grow and would sustain us through many years together. We would face times of laughter and tears, health and disease, overabundance and just scraping by, gains and losses. But one thing I always knew, when my Tom prayed with me for needs, we saw results. He knew His loving heavenly Father and he knew how to talk to Him. If we could just stand together in prayer, whatever the situation, it would all come out alright. It is so important for men to pray with their wives. The blessings of it are countless. Not only will it mean the world to her, but he will be amazed, as well. It will build the marriage, deepen their love for each other and bring wonderful security and unity in the Lord.

Tom had a saying and it went, "There's genius and stupidity in all of us". He didn't mind laying bare his own soul to share some of his 'not so stellar' moments, especially when he was preaching. One story that he shared many times over the years was when we lived in Colorado. We both worked in Denver but lived about 50 miles north, near Greeley. He got home before I did one evening and was hungry. Not wanting to wait until I got home to cook dinner, he decided to bake a small "Totino's type" pizza to hold him until something more substantial was prepared. He neglected to put the pizza on a pan, which would have been okay, except for the fact that he put the frozen pizza in, upside down….. As I came in the front door of the house, I was greeted by an unusual burnt smell and a rather guilty-looking husband. His words to me were, "Don't look in the oven. I'll clean it up."And he did, but he also made me promise not to tell anyone what he had done. I kept that promise until he repeatedly told the story on himself from the pulpit. Then I figured it was now public domain.

My Tom was so smart, so knowledgeable, and had great insight, except in the kitchen sometimes. He always beat me at monopoly or at jeopardy. It was so frustrating in college because I would study for a biology test for 5 hours and make an A. But Tom would listen intently in class, study for an hour and make an A. Someone could show him or talk him through making a project once, and he could do it the next time. I had to take notes and then be shown a couple of times for it to sink in. My Tom could fix almost anything, from replacing a car engine to hanging a ceiling fan. He would use the phrase "I'm a jack of all trades and a master of none". But that wasn't the case, for Tom could do just about anything he set his mind to. But most of all, my Tom could listen and he cared. No matter who was talking, whether a person of great importance and esteem, like the Air Force Base commander or simple down home folks, he listened. And by the end of the conversation, they knew that he cared. And isn't that what we all need from time to time, just someone to listen and to care?

Why the Lord has chosen to take this wonderful, smart, handsome, loving and caring man out of our lives, I don't know. But I do know that My Tom's Lord and Savior loves me and you more than we can ever imagine. So that must mean that God has a really good reason that we just don't see yet and we just have to trust Him and rest in Him, knowing that His plans for us are perfect.

Well Sweetheart, I know you have already been giving hugs & kisses to all our loved ones up there in Glory. Thank you for my final kiss last Saturday night. I look forward to the day when you will hold me once again in your tender, gentle arms. But until then, I'll rest in our Savior's arms and let Him relay your hugs.

I love you, sweetheart - Your Vonnie

Alone But Not Alone October 16, 2013

What is the one area that I've struggled with through all of my years? Being alone, abandoned, rejected, misunderstood, isolated. At the age of nine, my dad left me when my parents divorced. Oh I know that he didn't want to, that it broke his heart also to leave me behind. I know that he wasn't satisfied with our sporadic times together when he could make his way back to Dallas to spend a few hours or a day with me. I know that he wanted me to be a part of his life for more than one month each summer and the occasional holiday. I know all of that, now as an adult, but as a small child I just knew that I missed him. He was gone, he had left me, he was no longer close by to lift me high in the air and tickle me or hold me close and dance with me. I felt like a huge part of my young life was now gone. Don't get me wrong, I had a wonderful, loving mother. But before the divorce, I had two wonderful, loving parents. The void was there. But God gave me friends and family to help fill the empty place. And I realized during that time that He loved me and was always with me. That was when I publicly declared Jesus as my Lord and Savior.

Then as a teenager, I faced a situation where a lady that I respected and looked up to misunderstood something I had said. She berated and scolded me in front of all of my youth choir friends, unwilling to hear my explanation of the words I had spoken. Again I was heartbroken, felt abandoned, rejected, isolated and misunderstood. But this time, although deeply hurt, I determined to never do the same thing to another person. I would try my very best to give everyone the benefit of the doubt and hear them out. I have lived most of my life staying true to that promise. Again, although in a foreign country, with just a few friends to stand with me, I learned to draw near to the Lord for most of my comfort. It was during this time in my life, that I made my 'no matter what' pact with the Lord, and committed myself to living and singing just for Him.

As a young wife in my early 20's, I faced a time of fear and doubt when my husband went through eighteen months of unexplainable disease and pain. Hospitals, doctors, extra bills, disability and withdrawal were a part of daily life. We still prayed and read our Bible. We still went to church and tried to hold on to our beliefs. We felt alone, abandoned, rejected, isolated and misunderstood. Some of our friends judged us for our lack of faith. We still loved one another but there was a chasm between us because of the fear and uncertainty of the future. But as we continued to draw close to each other and God and tried to do those things that we knew were right, He intervened and brought the healing. It wasn't long after this that we answered the call to full time ministry.

And then in the midst of full time, vibrant ministry, we endured loss and injury that seemed devastating. It was a time of deep pain and soul searching, a time when we wondered if we would survive the depth of the wounds. How could we continue to minister when our world was so severely shaken. What had we done to deserve this pain? Were we at fault in some way? Could the Lord still use us to further His kingdom? There were so many questions, doubts and fears, so much uncertainty. Our entire world changed and we traveled through dark waters for many months. But then God showed us that we were not rejected, abandoned, misunderstood, isolated or alone. He revealed to us through a young lady singing a special song that our anchor still held and that He still held us. We began the process of forgiveness, healing and learning to trust again. And not too long afterward, ministry resumed also. He was still with us and doors opened up for us to continue His great work.

And now, after 40 years of marriage, my husband, Tom is gone. Spending all of those years making decisions and plans together, walking down life's road as two, I feel so alone. Half of me is gone. And yet I know that I'm not really alone, because my first love, Jesus, will never leave me and someday I will be reunited with my precious Tom. I try not to feel abandoned because I know I have many beside me supporting me and praying for me. The rejection tries to push its way in, but that also, I know to be a lie. I am highly favored of God, a precious child of the King. Misunderstood? Maybe sometimes, but I've learned to turn that over to my Lord. People will formulate their own ideas according to their own experiences and there's really no way to change that. So I've learned to let God and time fix it. If they are seekers of the truth, they will eventually realize their error. And then there's the Isolation. I can go through the dark cavern of isolation if I choose, hopefully I won't. It's MY choice. Friends and family are stepping up and supporting. They are calling or coming by, reaching out and offering help, giving hugs and kisses, writing sweet cards or notes on FB. Will it continue over the weeks and months? I'm sure it will because my physical and spiritual family are sensitive to the Holy Spirit and He will guide them.

As the days pass, the tears come more frequently and the challenges seem to increase but I know that with God and friends on my side, I'll make it through. I am so thankful for the love I feel and for their obedience to the nudges from the Lord. Although sometimes I feel very alone, I know that I'm not really alone after all.

Reflections of a Widow November 18, 2013

A widow, even the word seems strange to me. There are so many women who have already faced this season of life and I know that. It seems so strange to now be in that number. I still feel like a wife and I still feel married and yet I'm not? I've been a wife for more than 40 years and now that's changed? It just feels wrong. I know that the Lord is with me and He helps me every single day, so don't be worried for me. I'm really okay, it's just so different now.

Now I open the refrigerator and see a gallon jug of milk half gone and realize that it has been in there for over a week like that. I probably should throw it away. No longer are there Tupperware containers full of left-overs from the meals I've cooked. Now there are Styrofoam containers with left-overs from restaurants.

I get teary-eyed when I go to the store for supplies, because I no longer need to walk down every aisle looking for something new to fix for my hubby. I don't need the provisions as before because I won't be cooking much for myself. A small steak or chicken breast and a salad will suffice. Shopping for groceries is no longer fun unless one of the grandkids is with me or I'm helping Angela to buy food for her household. It all seems so bizarre. I have trouble walking through the men's department because sometimes I see something and I think, "That will look nice on Tom" and then I recall, with a stab of pain that I don't need it. It's so odd, this new place that I'm in.

Why didn't I realize how this would feel and everything that goes with a loss like this? And it is a loss, because even though I know right where Tom is, he's not here. Although I know I shall be with him again, I can't be with him now. And even though I know that our reunion will be glorious, I can't talk to him and have him respond to me. I'm not complaining, it's just so perplexing. This man that I've shared everything with, that I've leaned against and depended on is gone on a long, extended journey. No phone calls or e-mails. No facebook or skype. Not even a letter to share. But I know that I'm one of the blessed ones because our relationship was a good one and our years together were many. I was deeply loved and cared for by this wonderful man. I am truly blessed.

And then there are the times when I come home at night and just sit in the car, delaying the moment when I go into the empty house. It's a house that I love. It has everything in a home I've always wanted. It's a house that my Tom bought for me and remodeled for me. It's a place that the Lord led us to and when Tom saw how much I liked it, he found a way to buy it for us even though his original plan had been to buy it and flip it to make some money. And yet here I am sitting in the car for ten or fifteen minutes with my head back and my eyes closed. Once I get out and make myself go inside, I'm okay. I get busy doing what needs to be done.

And now, when I walk around my house and see everything that we've acquired through the years, somehow it looks different. It no longer seems necessary. Don't misunderstand, I'm thankful for everything, it's just that my outlook has changed. I think "What do I need all of this stuff for?" And yet I know that life will level out at some point and I WILL use all of these things again for family get-togethers. But for now it feels peculiar. These feelings are so unusual.

So when you get tired of doing the laundry and the daily cooking routine, be thankful that you have someone to do them for. When your house is a mess and you're at the end of your rope trying to keep up with it, try to be thankful that you have that special someone to pick up after. I've had all of those thoughts before and have tried not to complain because I knew that someday all the kids would be gone and I would miss the busyness. But I didn't expect to be alone in the house at this point in life. This is unfamiliar and unexpected territory for me.

I do find that I think about the Lord more. I talk to Him more consistently. I do have more time for my writing, sometimes not turning the TV on for days. I have additional time for my music and the Lord is giving me some new songs. If I have an idea in the middle of the night, I can get up and go to the keyboard or the computer and work on what He's giving me. There is good coming from this place that I'm in and I'm sure that it will get easier at some point.

I am also giving and getting more hugs these days. Tom always gave really good hugs and would just hold me close, especially if I was feeling down. I'm remembering to say "I Love You" more often when I talk to my family and friends. I'm thankful that Tom and I said those words fairly often, it's important you know. Don't take it for granted that you'll have tomorrow to say those special words or give that hug or kiss. It doesn't take that long, so do it today. And it feels really good whether you give it or receive it.

I find that I can function normally on less sleep than before, usually five or six hours. I always used to need right at eight hours not to feel tired. I'm thinking that all of the prayer on my behalf must be giving me an unusual level of strength and energy. I am so thankful that my hope and assurance is in the Lord. I shall see my Tom again someday and I shall see my precious Savior who continues to uphold and help this widow through her valley.

'Widow' – the word has taken on a new meaning now. I guess you can't really know how to prepare for this stage of life. But I am so grateful that I know the Lord personally, not just about Him, and He's staying close beside me. And I'm so thankful for friends and family who continue to show their love and support.

It has now been 14 weeks since my Tom went to Heaven. I find that I seem to be more unsettled than before. My emotions are more diverse and the changes in attitude and mood come more quickly, many times without warning. I'm told that this is normal but I don't like it. I don't like feeling out of control and weak and yet there's not much I can do but roll with it. Growing up and even into my 50's, I liked riding on rollercoasters. It was exhilarating and a thrill that would leave me laughing while gasping for air. You would think it would have prepared me for this ride I'm on now. One moment I'm on top of everything, trusting the Lord and speaking words of faith. The next moment I'm deeply sad, depressed and feeling helpless. This is such an unusual journey and season.

I don't grieve because I'm worried about Tom. He's great and having the time of his life, experiencing things that we can't even begin to imagine. The depths of love, joy and peace he must be feeling are beyond our finite understanding. The dimensions of sight, sound, feel, taste and even smell are beyond our earthly comprehension. Wow, I know he is reveling in the awe-inspiring beauty of it all because I've witnessed his reaction to the beauties of Colorado and Alaska. And I'm sure those pale in comparison to all that heaven is. The thought of what he is probably experiencing brings a smile to my face. I know that the Word says that there would be no tears in heaven, but I wonder if that means happy tears. I could always tell when a story or a scene touched Tom deeply because he would get teary-eyed and I would hear a sharp intake of breath and a sniff or two. He was very tender hearted, such a loving and compassionate man. And yet he was also very strong in so many ways.

My grief and sadness are selfish. I am the main focus of all that I feel these days. And somehow, that also doesn't seem right. So many have gone before me and yet I didn't understand the depth of their pain. I also grieve because I know that my children and grandchildren are hurting and missing Tom. I grieve because the little ones will never really know this incredible man. They are all so young. Oh sure, we will tell them stories and share funny things that happened. And maybe some of my stories will help them to know their "Wowo" better. I hope so. I pray that the spiritual seeds planted by my Tom will bloom and grow and that these children will grow up knowing his Lord and Savior, as he would want them to.

There are other changes, some not so bad. I no longer sit in the car a long time before coming in the house. I no longer worry about intruders, which was silly anyway, because Tom worked graveyards, so I was alone at night quite often. I do seem to panic a bit when something breaks or doesn't work properly. But when I think about it, that is also silly because I usually took care of the small repairs anyway. I didn't want to bother him with it when he was working long hours. I'm getting more use to eating out alone. Having a smart phone with facebook and texting helps fill in the gap of no conversation. We didn't usually discuss important issues over a meal out anyway. Those conversations were normally saved for night time when we were alone. I do miss being able to talk things over with him and getting his perspective. That always helped. And I miss us praying together at night for needs, friends and family. That was priceless.

My life still feels so uncertain. My future was always tied to Tom and what he wanted to do and felt led to pursue. And now, I'm not sure. But there are a few things that I do know. I am supposed to continue writing our stories, singing for the Lord at my church and with 'Appointed by Grace', love and support my family and friends. I feel compelled to reach out to my neighbors more than I have in the past. I also feel an urgency to get MY house in order. I'm in the process of having a will and a power of attorney drawn up. I need to downsize so that someday when the Lord sees fit to promote me to glory, my children won't have so much stuff to deal with. I guess when you have a major loss, you think of these things more seriously.

Before Tom left us, I didn't feel my age. I still felt like I could do just about anything I put my mind to. Now I look at myself differently. This experience has aged me some, I see it every morning. I've gained some of my weight back although I intend to turn that back around again. Sometimes I feel old now. And then I spend time with the Lord and He reminds me that age doesn't matter in a useful vessel and that sometimes maturity is a definite plus. And when I sing to Him and just worship, I feel so alive and a bit young again.

So here we are. My roller coaster jaunt is not over yet and probably won't be for a while. Maybe by the time things have leveled out again, I will have learned to enjoy and appreciate the ride and this process. I still know that whatever comes my way, God is on my side. He's working on my behalf, has a good plan and is for me, not against me. And by the way, that's true for YOU too. I hope that my sharing these thoughts and reflections have in some way offered you some hope and strength also. No matter what situation you're facing, your loving Heavenly Father has your back and is always close by. Read His Word, talk to Him, get to know Him better and lean on Him. You can trust Him to ride along with you and see you through to the end of your journey.

Further Reflections of a Widow
February 18, 2014

What to say now. I feel very alone although my children are close by. They are being very supportive even though I know that they are also missing Tom and hurting from the loss of his presence, voice, laughter, teasing, wisdom and tangible example. The pictures and memories are a comfort but they also bring a level of pain. We've already faced several 'firsts', Toms birthday was in November, then we went through the holidays. Valentine's day was quite difficult but tolerable because I was with friends.

The 'first' that got to me recently was a most unusual one, a church business meeting. These meetings are fairly calm and uneventful most years. Pastor Dale made some very kind and sincere comments about Tom because he had been a council member. That all went well. But about half way through the meeting, I realized how alone I was. Tom had always been by my side at these events, many times chairing them himself when we were Pastors. We had always discussed the issues, financial report and pending elections. And here I was with no words of wisdom and input from my husband, who was very discerning and who helped me to see a different side of things. After the meeting, I had a good cry in the bathroom, then pulled myself together and went home.

My grandson, Tony, has had a struggle that has been hard to watch. But we are trying to help him work through his loss. Tom, otherwise known to this little four year old as 'Wowo', was the only daddy Tony had for the first 3 ½ years of his life. We have explained to him that Wowo is in heaven with Jesus and that we will see him again someday. Tony will nod his head and repeat what we tell him and at night we will pray together, thanking God for Wowo and asking Jesus to please give him a hug for us. Tony likes to sit in Tom's chair and climbs on his riding lawnmower in the garage when I'm out there working. And this discerning child will come and pat me on the back or the arm and say 'Nana, you miss Wowo?' when he sees or hears me crying. Tony loves going to preschool but for the past two months, after Christmas break, he has struggled with us leaving him there. He will cry and struggle to follow us. We have started reassuring him that we will be back to get him, that we won't leave him there for long. It seems to be helping and he's not crying quite as much. The preschool teachers have been really good about working with us on this, trying to distract his attention and getting him focused on other things until he settles down. I guess that it's a process for all of us.

Today I had something happen that normally would have sent me into a panic. After helping Angela put the children in the car, I came back in the house only to find that my front door wouldn't close. I was preparing to go for an eye doctor appointment and couldn't possibly leave the house with the door unlocked much less open. It shut to within about half an inch of closing, but wouldn't completely shut. I examined the door and the frame to see if something was in the way, but couldn't see anything. The hinges looked okay and the frame looked just the same. When we walked out of the house it was fine, but now it just wouldn't close. I got my bag of tools and the step stool to look on top of the door thinking that maybe something had gotten caught up there, but it also looked normal. I laid down on the floor to look under the door and didn't see anything out of place. That's when I thought seriously about having a good pity party and cry. But then, I also thought about some conversations that the Lord and I had recently. He had impressed on my heart that he had stepped into that role as husband and would help me if I would allow Him to. Of course, at the time, I readily agreed saying "Okay Lord, it's You and me these days." And now those words came flooding back to me. Did I really mean them or was I just spouting off? So I sat up on the floor and said, "Okay Lord, it's You and me" and said a little prayer asking for His help. I calmly looked over the situation again, but this time I noticed the weather stripping on the bottom of the door sticking out past the edge of the door about an inch. I proceeded to use a screwdriver to try to remove it but then felt a check in my spirit. Was this the best way to handle the problem? The Lord spoke to my heart, try a hammer. So I dug the hammer out of my trusty tool bag and used it to pound the small strip back into place. The whole piece of stripping slid gently with each hit until all was back to normal. And guess what? The door shut smoothly just like it was supposed to.

Now, to any men out there reading this, you're probably wondering what the big deal was because you probably would have seen the problem immediately. But for me, in the past, if something didn't work or went wrong, I use to have a very handy and talented man around to take care of it. I didn't give it another thought but would hand it over to the expert. But now, I had to be the expert and I wasn't. Fortunately, I had the best handyman who ever lived whispering in my ear, my Jesus. I just needed to quieten myself down, not panic and listen more closely to his voice. It's a lesson that through the years I thought I had learned, but I guess I need another refresher course. I am truly thankful that I have the Lord in my life and know Him enough that most times, I can discern His still, small voice. Do you know Him like that? YOU CAN!! He loves each one of us the same and waits expectantly and eagerly for us to come to Him with our joys, sorrows, triumphs and problems. That refresher course that I spoke of earlier can be found in His Word and by just spending time with Him every day. It makes all the difference in the world and it's an Awesome way to live.

Reflections Once Again April 9, 2014

Six months have passed since Tom left us for Glory. How can this be? I still expect him to come through the door and yet I know that he won't. It seems that I can still feel him moving slightly in bed at night and then I realize that it's just my heart pounding. I still pick up the phone to call him but not as often. The waves of sadness are heavier now but don't seem to last as long. I'm still able to smile and joke and I look forward to spending time with people who make me laugh.

I'm not as lonely since the kids are with me. But I know that they need their own space so they can grow and develop as a family. And I need to adjust to being alone again. But it's been good to have them close for a while. I believe that this time has been beneficial for us all. But our time together in the same house is coming to an end and it's for the best. Perhaps I'm more prepared now.

I've also started some new activities and made some new friends. My neighbor, Elaine, is becoming a friend that I enjoy being around. I started going to water aerobics with her and met some other ladies who are widows. These friendships are developing as well. I started helping out with the food pantry at church on Wednesdays and feel good about this. I still may need to look at getting a part time job but I don't feel the urgency right now. I trust the Lord to open this door when the time is right.

I'm almost done recording my CD 'Consumed by Love'. Jason Rooks, who is in charge of it, has been wonderful through the whole process and is such an encouragement and support to me. He has taken my simple songs of worship and made them into works of art. I am so amazed by his talent and his willingness to pour so much of himself into this project. This is a dream that Tom and I have had for so many years. I never felt confident enough to pursue it until a few years ago. It was during the time that I worked for Dr. Barry Hughes and his wife Gail that I began to believe this dream was possible and began to really write my songs. We attended motivational chiropractic conferences that were very uplifting. And with Barry and Gail's support and friendship, I realized that God could and would use me to minister through the songs that He was giving to me.

And now I find myself writing a book, something I never even considered until recently. I should have known that when God spoke to my heart two years ago to start writing down our life stories, He had a definite purpose in mind. I have made a down payment to a publishing company to publish my book of short stories, poems and songs. I still have about fifteen to write and then I will compile everything and submit them for editorial review. I am NOT bored. In fact, I stay quite busy. I don't know how I could hold down a job and continue doing all that I do right now.

I still enjoy traveling and singing with 'Appointed by Grace'. These friends, Joe, Cindy, Karla, Brent and Rob have been such a wonderful support to me. They are so patient with my unexpected onset of sadness from time to time. They can usually sense it and are able to distract my thoughts to other things or find a way to make me laugh. They are also very sensitive to my need for silence sometimes. I am very blessed to have this great group of friends in my life.

I have had a couple of opportunities for solo ministry also. With my songs and stories, I have found a new venue where I can reach out and share. This has been a little unnerving since Tom and I were always a team. He did the preaching and I did the music and singing. It worked well for us but now I'm going it alone. Hopefully I can be effective in this ministry as well. I've never really been a preacher, although my children might disagree with that statement. I just want to do all that I can do for the Lord while I am able.

I am trusting the Lord to help me get my weight down again. I hate that I've gained in these last six months. The doctor thinks that it's my thyroid, so maybe I'll soon see a decrease of poundage instead of the increase, with a change in medication. The knees are pretty sore these days also and I groan a little when getting up out of the recliner. Is it the age?? I'm too young to slow down, I really don't have time to take it easy nor do I want to.

I'm actually doing my own taxes this year. Wow, what a milestone. Tom always did our taxes himself. I would just gather up all of the paperwork and receipts for him and he would take it from there. When I first considered having to do the taxes, it really worried me. But with the Lord's help and some kind advice from my friend Cindy, I'm making it through. And although very tedious, I believe it's going to be okay. Praise the Lord!!

It's very late and I need to stop all of this reflecting. As you can see, I'm okay. Thank you to all of my friends and family for the prayers and support. Thank you for the flowers, plants and money. Thank you to those who have been on hand to help in other ways, like fixing something on the car, helping the kids to move or replacing my roof at a reduced rate. So many have done so much to reach out and be Jesus with skin on. It truly touches my heart when I stop and consider each and every thing. Now don't get me wrong, I still need the prayers and support and probably will for quite a while. But as I said at the beginning of this journey, I am confident that my friends and family will continue to stand with me and pray for me. I was certain that the love and support would continue throughout the months and years. And I was right!!

A Stormy Sea
April 15, 2014

In the last few weeks I have faced days of extreme ups and downs, like trying to walk on top of a stormy sea. I have dealt with depression and sadness, wondering, at times, why I am still living when my dear husband is gone. And then within a few hours, my faith is boosted and revived. As I get my eyes back on the Lord, I see a great future ahead, full of service for the Lord. And then again I find myself wallowing in that sea of loneliness, grief and self-pity as situations and circumstances cause me to feel a strong sense of rejection. How unstable I seem to be. I have so much compared to most people and I am so very blessed. What's wrong with me that I can't remain steady out in this tempest and keep my eyes fixed on the Lord?

The enemy's lies bombard me from every side. Lies such as...

"The one person who totally loved and supported you is gone."

"You're alone and no one really cares about you."

"Things will never be the same, just give it up."

"God is finished with you, you're too old anyway."

"No one wants to hear anything you have to say, you don't know how to speak."

"Your singing is not what it used to be."

"Quit before you become an object of ridicule."

"People are just tolerating you because they feel sorry for you."

But I know that these are satan's lies that I hear and I take authority over those lies and vain imaginations in the name of Jesus because...

Greater is He that is in me than he that is in the world.

God has commended His love to me, in that while I was a sinner, Christ died for me.

Jesus said, "I will never leave you or forsake you."

The Word proclaims that I am the apple of His eye, the very center of His attention.

If I delight myself in the Lord, He will give me the desires of my heart.

now the plans I have for you,' declares the Lord, 'plans for not evil, plans to give you hope and a future."

do all things through Christ who strengthens me."

He has given me beauty for ashes and the oil (anointing) of joy for mourning.

Just acknowledging the lies and especially the truth helps me climb out upon the water again.

So how do we do it, my friends? How do we stay on top of that situation that weighs us down to within inches of hopelessness and despair? How do we see past the lies and deceit to the piercing Light of His Truth? We know the answer well, we just need a reminder. When the lies come and the sinister voices whisper, go to the Word of God. As I type these words and share with each of you, I gain renewed strength and assurance that looking to the Lord and dwelling in His presence is the answer. Speaking the truth (His Word) out loud puts the enemy and his lies to flight. I need to write out these Scriptures and post them on my mirror. Then they will be right in front of me and I can read them when the loneliness and depression crowd into my thoughts.

Thank You, Lord, for Your mercy, love and goodness to me, even when I momentarily forget about them and take my eyes off of You. May my focus and attention remain on You, Oh Lord, especially while I'm out in the midst of this stormy sea.

Reflections of the Past June 23, 2014

June 23rd marks a very special day in my life. Forty-one years ago today, I married my best friend and the love of my life. It was a lovely wedding in my home church of Bethel Temple Assembly in Dallas Texas. As with all weddings, the day held many specials memories from the beautiful rendition of 'The Lord's Prayer' by my cousin Jimmy to the violent shaking of our Pastor's hands as he served us communion and prayed over us. There was the tangible presence and promise of God Himself in the midst of that ceremony.

Who knew on that special day so many years ago where our lives would take us? Only the Lord! Together we would face the debilitating disease of Inflammatory Arthritis only to see the Lord's healing power take over when all seemed hopeless. We would travel through rain storms, sand storms, hail storms and blizzards. We would endure earthquakes in Alaska, wild fires in Colorado and run from a hurricane in Texas. We would work in a large church making enough money to save toward the future and then turn around and Pastor a very small church making hardly enough to scrape by on. We would see God step in and open doors for extensive ministry in the communities where we pastored, serving as town council member, mayor, EMT, air force chaplain, library board member, small newspaper journalist, postmaster and piano teacher. We learned how to acquire, butcher and package moose, caribou, halibut and salmon.

We learned a new culture and made lifetime friends when we became part of the Tlinget Indian community in Angoon Alaska. We witnessed the horrible blight of alcohol, drugs and immorality in people's lives and how destructive they are. We saw God move in the lives of men, women, teens and children bringing salvation, deliverance and many healings. We encountered the forces of darkness in ways that we never imagined and that many people have never seen or would believe if I were to share those stories. And we learned that greater is He that is in us than he that is in the world and that through God, all things ARE possible. This life that we began together so many years ago has been filled with so much, it's hard to believe. And for me, it's not over, there's still more to come.

My heart is full of thankfulness for all the years that we had together but it is also filled with a deep abiding ache as I go forward into the future without my Tom. I know that the Lord is with me and shall continue to guide, help and comfort me. However, today, my eyes are constantly full of tears as I remember that wonderful, smart, handsome and loving man that I committed my life to on June 23, 1973. Happy Anniversary Sweetheart!

Reflections on My Birthday July 25, 2014

It is one minute past midnight and today is my birthday. I've never had a birthday like today. As a child and teen, they were packed with the anticipation of presents, parties, goodies, hugs and kisses. As an adult they were filled with cards, phone calls, flowers, hugs and kisses. Sometimes they were anticipated and sometime they were dreaded. As the years have gone by, most have been anticipated with the expectation of an evening with family and friends, games and laughter.

But today is different, there will be hugs and kisses but not from my Tom. There will be friends and family, but not my Tom. There will be cards and maybe flowers but not from my Tom. My heart is so sad tonight, the weight of sorrow is so heavy. I made the mistake of watching the last hour of 'City of Angels' with Nicolas Cage and Meg Ryan. They fall in love and only have a short time together before she dies. At least I can rejoice in the fact that I had 40 years with my love and we shall be together again someday. But the movie has stirred up the grief that I keep buried much of the time.

I've always tried doing things my own way. I guess that I'm a bit of a rebel even though I try to get along with everyone and to accommodate people if I can. But if I can find a new road to take, I'll try it because I'm curious to see where it leads and if it's quicker or more interesting. I like to try new things and not necessarily follow the crowd. I enjoy being around other people, watching and listening to them. Sometimes I'm too quiet as I observe and have to make myself interact. However, these days, my quietness has become more pronounced. My thoughts drift to other days, to past regrets and to fond memories. I have a tendency to get caught up in my emotions and grief. I know that some people are probably thinking, 'She's starting to feel better now. The pain isn't as acute.' But that's not the case. I'm doing okay but I don't feel better. It's been almost ten months now and the pain is deeper and more easily rises to the surface. I find myself short tempered and angry sometimes and I don't like being that way. I find that I'm a little absent-minded also and that bothers me. But I'm sure it will all even out in time.

But on the brighter side, the Lord is VERY near. I hear His voice speaking to me quietly when I take time to listen. He is so close these days, it's amazing. His comfort and loving arms are definitely holding me. I know that I will survive, that somehow everything will work out. As Pastor Dale has preached lately, there's a day of Jubilee coming for me. A day of old debts being forgiven, of celebration and fulfillment. A day of promises and dreams becoming a reality. I must continue to hold on and to do those things I know are right and acceptable.

Tonight I grieve for my Tom, I miss him so much. His silly grin, the gleam in his eye when he's pursuing me for a kiss, his attempt at singing his version of the 'Happy Birthday' song, the way he laughs when he's chasing the grandkids, the stories that he would tell over and over again, the way his face lit up when a special program came on about Alaska or Colorado. These are good memories, though they still cause a sigh and an ache.

In the morning, it will truly be a new day. One filled with well wishes, friends and families. One filled with playtime with the grandkids and dinner with friends. It will be a good day even though it's a birthday that I would prefer not to have. Oh well, life DOES go on, doesn't it! And God has made it quite plain to me that He's not done with me yet. Sooo, I shall go to bed, cry a few more tears and perhaps dream of my Tom. Then I shall wake up to a new day of opportunity and following God's plan and purpose for my life, as it is now!

A Birthday Blessing
July 25, 2014

As I woke up this morning, I was determined to have a good day. I decided to quote one of my favorite scriptures to kick off the morning. Psalm 118:24 'This is the day that the Lord has made, I WILL rejoice and be glad in it.' It's a verse that Pastor Sheneman at Muldoon Community Assembly in Anchorage would speak quite often, as he burst through the church office door where we were working. It always blessed my heart and I have taken it for myself, especially if I'm feeling a little down.

Some of you may have been concerned after my musings last evening and normally I wouldn't post again so quickly. But I need to share the goodness of the Lord. After my initial, out loud, quote of that scripture, I went to my favorite chair and opened my Bible. What should I see there but Psalm118. I've never been very good with the location of scripture, so at first, I didn't realize that I was about to read the verse I had just quoted. Instead, my eyes landed on these verses. 'The Lord is with me, I will not be afraid. What can man do to me? The Lord is with me, He is my helper. I will look in triumph upon my enemies. It is better to take refuge in the Lord than to trust in man. It is better to take refuge in the Lord than to trust in princes.' And what's so amazing to me about opening the Word to those verses was the situation that I faced on this day. The business I needed to handle was rather complicated. It's not something I would normally take care of, Tom usually did. But it had to be done and I needed to address it as soon as possible and today was the day. Because of the scripture that the Lord led me to, I went into my day with the assurance that He had it all under control. Tom was not here to handle things but the Lord was. I had His promises firmly in hand and was able to go into a possibly difficult meeting calmly instead of nervously. Isn't God good!

And then all throughout my day, my friends and family continuously sent words of love and support wishing me a Happy Birthday, speaking words of comfort and encouragement. Today was a good day. There were hugs, kisses, cards, presents, cupcakes, homemade chocolate chip cookies, a swim date with my grandson and dinner with friends.

I'm so glad that even though I woke up feeling down, I decided to rejoice in the Lord and then take the time to allow Him to speak into my life through His Word. I faced a busy day and could have been side-tracked so easily. I'm thankful that I listened to that still small voice that called me to come dwell with Him for a while and that I heeded that nudge to go into the secret place with my dearest friend. And I'm grateful to all of my friends, who followed the Lord's leading, to speak words of reassurance and caring. Despite me missing my Tom and because of special friends and the Lord, THIS HAS BEEN A GOOD DAY AND A BLESSED BIRTHDAY!!

Reflections and Milestones August 4, 2014

Today I reached a milestone! To many it will seem silly, but for me it brought a sense of achievement. I have never needed to know how to mow a lawn and I'm sure that I'm not the only one. I thought that I could figure it out if it ever became necessary. Living here in Texas and in Colorado, that was an area that Tom always handled. For much of our time in Alaska, it wasn't an issue at all. When we were in Anchorage, we either lived in an apartment or in a house that the church provided and the mowing was taken care of. In Bethel, we were only there in the winter so only dealt with snow. When we lived in the Tlinget Indian village of Angoon, we didn't have a yard. The church and parsonage were right on the water, so our back yard was a beach. In Anderson Alaska, we did have a yard but there again, Tom handled the mowing. And since the summers were rather short, there was only about three months that the grass grew.

For some time now, I have struggled with getting our riding lawn mower working properly. Every time the yard needed mowing, something seemed to go wrong or be messed up on it. Once, my neighbor took pity on me and mowed for me and another time I hired a someone to take care of it. But I don't want to hire it done if I don't have to. I have a decent mower, I am quite capable of taking care of things and I'd rather spend my limited income on other necessities. Twice before, Oscar Warner from my church, Brazoria 1st Assembly, has come over and worked on it and even mowed for me. But once again, I was faced with the unknown. I had been told that the battery was bad, so I bought a new one expecting that to fix the problem. However it didn't. There was no spark, no sound, no indication of any life in that mower. So reluctantly, I spoke to Oscar to ask for his help again. No one else could figure out what was wrong. And as usual, he came by to help. But this time, I was home and he was able to give me a 'Mower 101' class. Ladies, did you know that a mower won't start if the lever for engaging the blade has been left on? And did you know that to start a mower, you need to be sitting on the seat or at least pushing down on the seat because that's how the connection with the battery is achieved? I didn't know these things until today. I now have a mower that works and that I understand how to operate. Tonight, right before sundown, I mowed my yard. WooHoo!! I was very dirty and quite sweaty when I was done, but I DID IT!!

Now don't get me wrong, I have a son and a son-in-law that are more than willing to mow for me. However with their schedules and the fact that the mower has been so persnickety, things just haven't worked out for them to do it recently. I'm sure they will take over for me now, but it feels really good to know that if I need to do it, I can. Now if I can just figure out how to get my swimming pool cleared up!

And we faced another milestone today. It had always been a tradition with Tom (Wowo to the grandkids) to give Tony a ride on the mower after the mowing was done. So tonight was a happy time for my grandson, who misses his Wowo so much. We were able to revive the tradition that was always such a fun-filled time for Tony and his grandpa, but this time Nana was able to get in on the fun.

But before closing, I want to extend a special thank you to Oscar for his kindness and help. He is such a gentle and patient man to put up with all of this and to teach this not-so-old dog some new tricks. Thank You so much Oscar!!

A Widow's Heart
August 14, 2014

The stress test is done! My heart is in good shape! Now don't get me wrong, this was not your regular, run of the mill, stress test. So maybe it doesn't count. But to me, I passed it! Over the past several months, I've had some doubts about how my heart was doing. Since Tom was promoted to Glory, I seem to have had more physical aches and pains. There was a period of time when I was always tired and felt run down. Even just getting up out of my recliner seemed harder. I guess it's all part of the grieving process.

But on the morning of August 14, 2014, I found out that the 'ole ticker' was still working pretty good, even with my occasional irregular heartbeat. I was scheduled to catch a 6:15am flight to go to my nephews wedding in Canada. I had it all planned out in my head. In order to get there early and have a leisurely time at security and going through the airport, I would wake up at 4am, leave about 4:45am, right? NOT!! The airport is an hour drive from my home. As Angela and I turned onto the airport's main thoroughfare, I looked at the clock and realized it was 5:45 and that my flight would leave in thirty minutes.

As the panic began to formulate I said, "Oh Tom, this never would have happened if you were here!! You always kept me on track." Talk about stress and the adrenaline kicking into high gear!! The outside baggage check had ten people in line, so I ran inside to the ticket counter and express checking. "Oh good", I thought "only four people ahead of me." The clock was ticking and my hands were beginning to shake a little. I pulled my phone out to scan the bar code on my electronic boarding pass. It wouldn't scan! The ticket attendant, kindly smiling at me, gently and calmly turned my phone around and it went through! She quickly checked my bag but tentatively informed me that it might not make it onto that flight.

"Dear Lord, it's in Your hands, but I have to get on that plane!" I prayed, as I hurried to my next checkpoint.

I went to security knowing that since I checked in early, on-line the day before, that I should go through express. The man directed me to the longer line. I explained that my plane was leaving in eighteen minutes, so he asks for my boarding pass. Not thinking clearly, I handed him my baggage claim since it's the only paper I had. He directed me back to the ticket counter to get a boarding pass. As I turned to rush back, I remembered, it's on my phone! By this time tears were beginning to form in the corners of my eyes and my hands were shaking violently. I showed him my phone and he allowed me to pass to express boarding.

At security, I pulled out my phone for them to scan the bar code but I was shaking so badly that the man had to take it from me to scan it. Thank the Lord for kind, compassionate people! I made it through security and started running down the hallway of the airport. Well.... maybe not running, but walking very swiftly, heart racing and shaking all over. And all the time, wishing my strong and steady husband was by my side, encouraging me forward.

I heard an announcement calling my name, "Revonne Behrend, please proceed immediately to gate 43, your flight is departing shortly". I could see gate 43 in the distance. There was one person standing at the still open door. I arrived panting yet relieved and he quickly scanned my phone then escorted me down the companionway. It was 6:10am. I made it!!! Thank you Jesus!! Now, what do you think? Did this ordeal count as a stress test? God is good!! Although Tom couldn't be by my side, the Lord certainly was. I would make it to the wedding and The Lord willing, I wouldn't have to wear my blue jeans to the ceremony. I was praying that my bag would arrive safely also!

I made the rest of the trip with no more incidents. Our landing into Chicago Midway Airport was a little bumpy but we were fine and on time. My gate for the next leg of my journey to Buffalo New York was only about 200 yards away and I was able to relax and charge my phone while waiting. The flight to Buffalo was quite enjoyable with a flight crew that was rather perky and humorous. After the doors were secured and everyone was seated, the flight attendant made her first announcement "Did anyone drop a brown wallet?" Everyone on the aircraft looked up, scanning the other passengers to see who may have done this. Then she said "Now that we have your attention, we will proceed to our airline safety guidelines." She continued giving the demonstration of how to buckle the seatbelt, etc. Then she began to talk about the no smoking rule. "Since smoking is prohibited on our aircraft, if you are caught smoking in the lavatory, we will assume that you are on fire and will take appropriate action." She then directed us to the oxygen mask. "If there's a loss of cabin pressure, an oxygen mask will drop down in front of you. To breathe into your mask just deposit a quarter for the first minute and each minute after that is on us." And "If traveling with a child or someone who acts like one, please secure their mask first and then yours. If traveling with more than one child, you might want to pick your favorite now, in case you don't have time to get to both." Then when talking about an emergency landing in water, she said "To inflate your flotation device, just breathe normally into the red tube. If you don't know how to breathe normally, breathe like this (she then proceeded to breathe in a slow, sexy manner) then said "That's my favorite part of this talk." "Once you are in the water, the rest is up to you, paddle, paddle, paddle till you reach the shore." At the end of the announcement, "If there's anything we can do between Chicago and Buffalo to make your flight more enjoyable, please let us know in Buffalo. And finally, "If you want to check your emails or go online, there is an $8.00 fee. It's a really good thing to do and we encourage you to keep in touch with your family and friends this way. Plus, it helps our bottom line." The flight from then on was pleasant and the crew was very nice and friendly. At the end of the flight, after landing in Buffalo, she came back on the intercom to say "Please stay seated with your seat belts securely fastened until Captain America turns off the seat belt sign." Also, "Make sure to take all of your carryon items with you or you can come find them at my garage sale next Saturday." And finally, "Thank you for choosing our airline for your travels. You could have made another choice but definitely not a better choice."

Now don't you appreciate people with a sense of humor? That day started out very stressful but this crew surely brought a sigh of relief, a smile and even outright laughter to lighten my load. My Tom would have enjoyed it thoroughly, finding a way to banter back and forth with the crew and perhaps give them some new ideas for future comments and jokes.

And to top off my travel experience, my suitcase was faithfully waiting for me on the conveyor belt in baggage claim. I didn't have to search through all kinds of bags, waiting anxiously to see if it had made it through. There is was, prepared for its retrieval. Thank the Lord!

So I made it and had a wonderful visit with my siblings, nieces and nephews. I didn't have to wear my blue jeans to the wedding and although it was a very long day, it was a very good day. We had an enjoyable wedding rehearsal and a delicious dinner with lots of stories and laughter. Pictures were taken, kisses were stolen, prayers were spoken and hugs were given. The bride and groom were radiantly happy and apparently very much in love. All was as it should be for two people beginning a lifetime together.

As I reflected back on another wedding more than forty years earlier, I could smile. The memory brought a dull ache to my heart, several bittersweet tears and much thoughtful reflection. But it also inspired a prayer for my nephew and his lovely bride, that they too would have as many blessed years together as Tom and I had.

This vacation began as a test for my heart but ended with a heart full of gratitude.

Reflections and Memories September 18, 2014

Two weeks from this coming Sunday, it will have been a year since Tom left for heaven. In some ways it seems so long ago and then it seems like yesterday. I can still vividly remember the Doctor's face as I rushed off the elevator heading to my husband's room. They had phoned me earlier, telling me that the nurse called for a code blue and that they were trying to revive him. I had hoped that the steps they took had worked and that they were able to stabilize his heart. But when I saw the Doctor's face, I knew. The anguish of the message he had to deliver was written all over his features. They couldn't save him. They tried seven times to revive him. They were so sorry for my loss. The words seemed to come from somewhere else. Surely this was just a nightmare and I would wake up. But No, my friends, Joe, Cindy and Karla stood close by, ready to help with whatever I needed. And there in front of me stood Tom's cardiologist. The compassion that I saw in his eyes helped me, as I braced myself for the image of my husband lying lifeless on the hospital bed.

When I walked into the room, everything was in place and peaceful. Tom appeared to be sleeping. It would have been so easy to convince myself that he was just resting except for the fact that there was no snoring going on and no little twitches. Those two things were always a part of his sleep habit. I took his hand in mine, it was still warm. I brushed back his hair and stroked his beard over and over again, as though the motion would wake him up. But I knew it wouldn't. I stayed beside him like that for about an hour until more people arrived. Then I would greet them, give hugs, and then turn back to Tom. Finally after a while, I realized that the warmth was leaving his body. I caught myself rubbing his hand a little harder as though that would help retain the heat, but I knew better. Then at last, I gave up, knowing that nothing I did would make a difference. He was gone, he had left me. I'm sure that he didn't want to, because he had always made sure that I was taken care of. But never the less, he was now with Jesus, my parents and grandparents. He was experiencing the magnificence of Glory and the fullness of dwelling with the Lord. It was a brand new dimension of existence. This life was over, his race had been run and he had finished his course. I knew that I would see him again someday, but not for a while.

Now, I just have to figure out how to complete my race without him by my side. I had forty years of love and adoration, of knowing that at least one person on this earth thought I was beautiful even as my weight fluctuated and more wrinkles appeared. I had a man of honor and integrity that I could look up to and depend on. I knew that he was true to me and never lied to me. Problems were shared and solutions were discovered together. The world could turn against me, but I was assured that Tom would always stand by me. No matter what came, we stood as partners, united.

At first, I looked at this separation as temporary, and in a way it is. I thought, "it's like he's on a long journey to a place where there are no telephones. It's like those men who had to go off to war for years at a time with no means of communication." Perhaps this attitude and thought process kept me from dealing with the full impact of my loss for a while. Maybe it gave me time to adjust to the loss. Was I hiding from the truth, should I have handled it differently? I don't believe so, only God knows for sure.

One thing is certain, the support and prayers of my friends and family has helped me tremendously as I've moved through these months of change and new challenges. The past year has proven to be very educational and humbling. I've learned that it's okay to ask for help. I've learned how to do things I'd never done before, like filing a tax return, mowing the yard and cleaning our swimming pool.

But with all of the change and new adjustments, you would think that it would be easier, and in some ways it is. However, the loneliness and the depth of my loss are much more evident now. I miss him more than ever and grieve over seemingly silly things.

This summer has held some special events that have evoked many smiles and tears, sometimes within minutes of each other. In August, I was able to attend my nephew's wedding in Canada. It was such a special event where I was able to spend time with my siblings and family. The wedding was beautiful with lots of teasing and laughter, hugs and kisses. The reception was also quite enjoyable but evoked very mixed emotions on my part. As the bride and groom danced their first dance together as husband and wife, I smiled thinking how precious the sight was. And then I cried because I couldn't dance with my Tom. As the groom swept his bride into a low swoop to kiss her decisively, I laughed with delight. And then I cried a few quiet tears because I missed those special kisses. I loved the twinkle that I saw in the grooms eyes as he reached for his bride for another kiss. And then I remembered the twinkle in Tom's eyes when he would come to me for a kiss. Those eyes never lost that gleam. It was there when we were young and still there a year ago, when we kissed goodnight at the end of our final day together, not knowing it would be our last kiss. So you see, the wedding, although a happy and joyful time, stirred up memories and some pain.

And then there was the Stewart family reunion. It was a fun time of eating, drinking, visiting and singing. Many of the people I knew, many I did not know. While watching all of the festivities, I realized that I felt very alone. If Tom had been there, he would be telling me who everyone was and would be visiting with many, sharing some of his favorite stories. I would have stood close by, only halfway listening, because I had heard the stories many times before. I would have been content to let Tom carry the conversation as we spoke with different family members, with just an occasional comment from me. He truly enjoyed talking to people and catching up on their life and activities. When the singing began, he would have proudly urged me forward to go sing a couple of songs and then bragged on me to whoever was close by. He was my biggest supporter and thought that I never hit a bad note and didn't seemed to notice when I did make a mistake. As I sat there, I thought about these things. And even though I did go forward to sing a couple of songs and was greeted very warmly and received encouragement, it just wasn't quite the same. I was missing my Tom.

And now today, I attended a friend's funeral. She was such a sweet lady, who was also a widow. Barbara lost her Charles back in 2007 and I could tell how much she missed him. When we would take her home from church or go out to dinner with her, she would speak of her Charles and reminisce about their years together. I really didn't understand the level of loss she was experiencing until a year ago. Tonight, her home-going stirred up my grief. I was thinking that she is reunited with her Charles. But also, she is getting to see my Tom and visit with him. They always seemed to have a lot to talk about and I don't begrudge her that. I just miss not being able to talk to him.

Now, why am I disclosing all of these thoughts and reflections with you? Why do I bare my soul and reveal my innermost feelings.

I'm normally a very private person and don't always open up as much as I should. I feel that I'm supposed to share with you all, my friends. Perhaps my musings will help someone who is experiencing the same thing. Maybe a friend or relative is going through some of these emotions and my sharing will help you to understand a little bit of what they are dealing with. If these writings accomplish that, then I'm content. As you can see, I am enduring. I'm making it through. I do appreciate your prayers, though. It seems that this one year anniversary is affecting me more than other events have. Thank you for the continued love and support. And please keep the prayers coming.

Reflection's Journey November 6, 2014

One year and one month ago today, my life changed forever. At first I was caught up in the preparations of a funeral and paying honor to my Tom. Then I worked through all the paperwork and details of insurance, death benefits, social security interviews and such. Holidays and special events came and went, weighed down with memories and pictures flashing through my mind. Some brought tears and others brought smiles. But during these first six months of change and adjustments, I seemed to be enveloped in a cushiony cloud, floating along without too much heavy grief.

Then April came and late night sleeplessness and tears. Although the Lord was still very near, the cloud was gone and the cushion with it. Busy days and attentive friends helped but the nights were sometimes brutal. Pitfalls of desperate hopelessness laid in wait for me at every turn and I had to stay very aware and careful to avoid them. The enemy seemed intent on dragging me down with accusations, lies and vain imaginations. I had to fight to keep my attitude and thinking headed the right direction. But with the Lord's presence, help and assurance that there was a reason for it all, I made it through that phase. His plan was beginning to take shape. Maybe there could be life, ministry and purpose separate from my beloved Tom.

Summer held special events and trips that turned my focus back to the plan that God had for my life now. Doors seemed to open and new ministry began. Our dream of my own CD with my original songs was completed and in my hands. Plans and preparation for writing the book about our life and concentrating on its completion, helped to keep me focused in a positive manner. The stories that I wrote and expanded on for the book helped to bring a level of comfort in my grieving. As I spoke and shared with others about our life together and how God's presence and intervention played a vital role, I was reminded of God's ability and intention to see me through any and all situations.

My grieving took on a more healthy and normal tone. More and more, I began to see other women who were widows and recognized the signs of grief in them. My prayer life took on a new urgency to pray for these ladies and especially for the newly widowed. I also became aware of friends facing terminal illness with their mates. My attention was drawn more away from my own feelings to the feelings of others and what they were facing. And I realized that I am one of the blessed ones, to have had such a good marriage and forty years of fairly consistent, happy memories.

These thirteen months have held many ups and downs. I'm sure these experiences are very natural for someone who loves and trusts the Lord and is in my season of life. However, the one year anniversary has proven to be the most difficult time yet. Again, I have had to battle vain imaginations, insecurities and doubts about my purpose and abilities. But now I'm going to the Word quicker, turning on Praise music more consistently, staying in a fairly constant attitude of prayer and separating myself from negative attitudes more readily. I'm coming through it and fortunately it's happening a little quicker this time.

There are two songs that I have heard recently that have played an important role in helping me to deal with my life as it is now. They are "You're gonna make it" and "Tell your heart to beat again". Both have touched me deeply and caused me to think more clearly about things. I hope to sing them as an encouragement to others someday soon.

I can see glimpses of daylight now. I miss my Tom more than I could have ever imagined but at the same time I have the feeling that it's going to be alright. I have absolutely no desire for a new relationship, but sometimes the loneliness is so heavy that I feel almost suffocated. But I know that will pass away or at least ease eventually. I miss so much about my Tom, especially his hugs and the special look of love I would see in his eyes. I miss his corny jokes and endless stories about Alaska. I miss seeing his interaction with the grandkids. And Tom always picked out the most beautifully written cards for my birthday or anniversary. The scripture that talks about 'the two shall become one flesh', is so true. I knew that we had a deep abiding love for one another. But I had no idea how very deep it went and the level of wrenching and ripping away that would come with the separation of death.

I wonder sometimes if this level of pain was experienced by my mother when she went through the divorce from my dad. I think there must be some similarities and perhaps even more acute pain because of the feelings of rejection and betrayal that sometime accompany divorce. I mention this to make us aware of the need to pray and love people through these events. Don't hesitate to give a hug, invite them to lunch or a movie, or just make a phone call or send a card. All of these gestures have been such a blessing and help to me over the past thirteen months. When you feel that nudge from the Lord, don't delay but act upon it right then. The Lord brings the healing but most of the time He uses us in the process. Wow, what an honor, to be used by God to bring healing. Thank you to all who have reached out to me over the past year. Your expressions of love have made a difference and the healing has begun. I still have a ways to go and according to many friends who are further down this path, it will continue for some time to come. Probably until we are all reunited in Heaven. But in the meantime, God is Good and will see us through. 'I'm gonna make it' and 'I'm telling my heart that it's okay to beat again'.

Reflections of Thanksgiving
November 28, 2014

Today was a nice day. It started out at home with the kids and grandkids, cooking breakfast, watching parades on TV and hanging Christmas lights. Then in the afternoon, we traveled to Houston to meet with family for Thanksgiving dinner. The day was topped off with even more family as we all came together for various desserts. The kids played together and sang Christmas songs. The adults talked, catching up on the details of our lives. There were many smiles and some tears but much laughter. We shared and reflected on how God had brought us through various situations and how He had miraculously intervened in some cases. It was truly a time of gratefulness and thanksgiving.

When you earnestly look back over a year and review the events of those twelve months, you become abundantly aware of God's presence and interaction in your life and the lives of those you care about and love. It seems like I forget a lot of what God has done for me though. I don't always recall the little blessings that, at the time, were instrumental in turning my day around. What if I started to chronicle each event where God stepped in to save a life, or perhaps when He gave me a special revelation or blessing? What if I began to jot down those times when an answer to prayer came unexpectedly or maybe an unintentional solution presented itself before I even ask? What about those days when friends or family made my day with a special deed or word and somehow it was just when I needed it the most. What would next Thanksgiving look like if I kept a Thanksgiving Calendar, where each day I wrote down a blessing or God-moment from that day? It doesn't have to be elaborate, just a few words as a reminder. I have a feeling that next year would be filled with even more celebration and gratefulness.

I think that this is something I need to implement. Then on those days when I'm feeling sad and down in the dumps, I just need to look at that calendar and review all of the blessings from previous days. At those times when I feel all alone and like no one cares, I can review the past and recall the times someone called, sent a card or just a text. Maybe it would help me to keep my attitude on track and silence the lies of the enemy. It is good to be reminded of the love and faithfulness of the Lord and His people. Sickness, loss and trials will come in this life, it's inevitable. I want and need to figure out how to keep my eyes fixed on the One who loves me the most. I need to be reminded of the love and support of family and friends.

How about it? A Thanksgiving Calendar? I think I'm going to try it, what about You? Join me?

Christmas Hope and Reflections
December 23, 2014

*"It's the most wonderful time of the year. With the
kids jingle-belling and everyone telling you, be of good
cheer. It's the most wonderful time of the year."*

To be honest, I haven't been able to listen to that song all the way
through this year. After just a few stanzas, I find myself changing
to another radio station. And I'm one who loves Christmas music.
Most of the songs don't bother me and I still enjoy and even sing
along with them, but that one hits a nerve.

Don't get me wrong, I love Christmas and all of the good will
and smiles on people's faces. I delight in the excitement of the
children as they anticipate presents and countdown the days until
Christmas morning. I enjoy the glow in their eyes and squeals of
delight when you drive down a street with oodles of Christmas
lights and Holiday Blow-ups. I'm enchanted with all of the
Christmas programs and activities filled with drama and music.
I appreciate the kindness of a stranger who allows you to pull
out in front of them when you're in holiday traffic and frustrated
because many others ignored your dilemma. I find satisfaction in
all of the Christmas movies that are geared to give you a good, old-
fashioned, happy cry.

Let's face it, it IS the most wonderful time of the year, as we
celebrate God's amazing gift to mankind, Jesus Christ. But, truthfully,
it is also a very sad time of year for so many people. People who are
struggling with severe pain and disease, perhaps confined to a
hospital bed. Those who are homeless or facing eviction because
of a lost job. The numerous elderly who are all alone for various
reasons. Or those who have faced a devastating loss of a loved one
or close friend. I honestly don't know how people survive the death
of a faithful life-long spouse without the Lord and His people there
to comfort and support them. The holidays this year have been so
much more difficult for me. The weight of grief and loneliness has
pulled me down to the edge of despair and depression like I've
never known in all my life. I function well for several days and then

something will happen and I'll be thrown into a pit of ap
hopelessness. And there I remain for several hours up to a c
of days. My family and friends remain close by. But even in their
midst, my mind tries to play tricks on me. I relive all of the things I
could have done better as a wife. My mistakes and failings seem to
be magnified. My abilities and purpose in life seem to be nullified
and belittled, making me think that all I attempt to accomplish in
my life now, is in vain.

It appears that my life is also over, why push on? But push on I
must and I do.

Thank the Lord for His Word and for gospel music with sound
messages of hope and truth. Praise the Lord for Pastors with a
timely message from God on a Wednesday night and for their
willingness to share that Word even though the crowd is small
and some might not understand or appreciate it. Thank God for a
church family from several different denominations, who respond
to the nudges of the Lord to reach out in some small and seemingly
insignificant way. Their obedience to His still, small voice helps to
bring a smile, where there had been many tears. It brings a feeling
of acceptance where rejection and loneliness had been seeping in.
And it helps to silence the lies of the enemy and allow the Truth to
be embraced again.

I realize that by posting this, I reveal my weakness. I admit to
the struggle to keep my thoughts and attitudes on track. As a strong
mature Christian, I should have it all together and never waver,
right? But let's face it, we all waver at some point. Why would we
need faith, if we were in control and had the firm answer in hand at
all times? How would we mature in the Lord if there weren't trials
and problems to overcome and persevere through? So maybe my
transparency will help someone else who is battling loss and all of
the emotions that go with it.

If you are facing similar issues, stay in the Word, faithfully
attend church, keep busy and remain close to your family. When
you feel like curling up in a ball in the back of your closet - take a
flashlight, a pillow and your Bible with you. That way, you won't
stay in there too long. Christmas IS a wonderful time of year, and
along with the tears and grief there can be joyful and fun times.

Thank you Lord for being willing to come to this earth and take
on human form. You did this in order to know, firsthand, the depth

of feelings and difficulties that we all face from time to time. And through YOUR struggle from the manger to the cross, You provided a way for us to be reconciled to God, our Heavenly Father.

Tis the Hope and Reflection of Christmas.

Reflections of Choices Made 1-20-15

Yesterday I received a letter that made my day much brighter. It was already a beautiful, warm day. My grandson Tony was out of school for the Martin Luther King holiday. We were having an enjoyable day working around the house and doing various chores. The temperature was a pleasant 66 degrees as Tony helped me brush and scoop leaves out of the swimming pool. When Angela returned home, she brought in the mail and handed it to me. While Tony, all decked out in swim trunks, water wings and cowboy boots, played with his T-ball and bat, I sat down to look through the pile of letters. There was one in particular from a company called Life Gift. I had already, over the last year, received a few letters of gratitude, condolences and informational letters, informing me of their continued activities. This was the company that had handled the organ and tissue donations from my Tom. I had signed papers at the hospital on that fateful day giving them permission to retrieve and utilize portions of Tom's body to help others in need. Tom and I had discussed this several years before and had shared our desire to be organ donors. A few times over the years, as we got older and the joints got a little stiffer, he jokingly mentioned his doubt that, when the time came, that they would find anything left of much use.

And now on this pristine, spring-like day, I opened a letter from a young 22 year old woman. She shared with me and our family her sincere thanks and appreciation for our 'generous gift'. She sweetly offered her condolences at our loss and then began to share her story. When she was 14, she had damaged a ligament in her knee causing it to unexpectedly dislodge quite often. As the years went on, the injury became worse, to where she could no longer run or do any activities because of the fear of pain and dislocating that knee. She had recently become an aunt of a little girl who was already walking, even running. She indicated that Tom's gift had given her the opportunity to keep up with her niece as she began to grow. And for that, she was very thankful. Being able to take part in the child's life, in every way, meant the world to her. She had come to the conclusion that, tomorrow is not guaranteed for anyone and we need to cherish every moment and every memory with those we love. She had her surgery in the beginning of August and after a month of rehab and recovery was already walking. She was looking forward to being fully recovered and able to run after her niece. Then she planned to return to college and get her degree to become a teacher. It had been her goal in life to teach children and to make a positive impact in their lives and their education. She strongly felt that all of this was possible because of the organ donation from my Tom.

As I read the letter, I had to stop a few times since the words blurred together because of bittersweet tears that gathered in my eyes. I'm glad that we made that choice together and that this young woman would have a new lease on life because of it. But there was so much more to the story. I intend to write my own letter and share that story with her at some point. It's so interesting to me the way that God works and how He can bring things around in a full circle.

It was at the age of 22 that Tom was stricken with a disease called Inflammatory Arthritis. After many doctors visits and three different 9-day stays in hospitals, over an eighteen month time period, he was barely able to walk. He had to quit his full time job as a machinist and had to quit his full time load of college classes because of the debilitating illness. The pain in the ankles, knees, a hip, low back, a shoulder and a jaw were so excruciating that he could hardly function. He could only get around on crutches and was preparing to get a wheelchair. Tom was quickly accepted on disability and was informed that there was no cure, only pain management with twelve aspirins each day. However, God had other plans. After all of those months of struggling with this crippling disease, his complete healing came and he was able to resume life, go back to work and graduate from college.

And now, ligaments from one of those previously crippled and God-healed knees was restoring health and healing to another 22 year old. How incredible is that!! Tom would be so pleased! And most likely would be cracking a few jokes as he boasted about his old ligaments being useful in a young body. I can see the twinkle in his eyes as he would hunch his shoulders and have a good belly laugh. I'm so glad that someone else has been added to the long list of people who were touched and changed for the better because of the special man that I married so many years ago, my Tom.

Thank You Lord for Your continued blessing and for giving us all another reason to rejoice and smile as we walk through this valley of loss. YOU ARE SO GOOD!!

Reflections of Grief 3-19-15

The last few months have been filled with long periods of sadness and grieving. The more time that goes by causes me to miss my Tom more than ever. I long to see that twinkle in his eyes again, to feel his arms around me for an unexpected hug, to hear his snore or corny jokes. Of course, I don't dwell on the difficult times that all couples face, only the good and happy times. When you're in the midst of a 40 year relationship, you take so many things for granted. And part of you realizes that you are very fortunate and blessed to have a good marriage but it's a part of everyday life. Somehow, you expect it to go on forever and don't really think it will come to an end. But as we all know, life changes and we all face new seasons. Through it all, God is good, faithful and always present.

Dealing with everyday problems now seems magnified. Before, the buck stopped with Tom but now it stops with me. But there again, I have learned that the Lord is a very present help in time of need. I'm amazed at how He continues to guide, help and provide as I face situations and circumstances on my own.

There is one area that I am struggling to hand over to Him and let go of. All through my life, I have fought to control my weight. I have tried almost every diet out there, checked out different supplements, energy drinks, weight loss meals and shakes, cleanses, etc. The result is always the same, I lose for a while then I gain again. Before Tom died, I had lost 25 lbs. and was very pleased that I finally seemed to have things under control. But since his death, I have gained 20 of those pounds back and nothing I try seems to help slow down the upward progress. I am very conscientious about eating healthy, consuming smaller quantities of food, drinking lots of water, avoiding sugar and fried foods. My overall diet lately has been fruits, vegetables and lean meats. Now don't get me wrong, I do give into temptation occasionally. I will have a real coke or piece of candy from time to time. I allow myself to have a piece of cake or a couple of cookies at special events. But those times are few and far between, not really enough to keep me in this upward spiral. I have been known to be very naughty with my diet, but those years are long past. No longer do I eat an entire Sara Lee Cheesecake because I am ashamed at how big a slice I took and didn't want my new husband of less than a year to know what I had done. So what to do? What to do? I must obey that still small voice and let go of the stress. Most likely that's the culprit. The stress, grief, medications and hormones are playing havoc with my body. But there again, God is faithful and will help me to know what path to take. He will guide me to the truth and obedience to His voice. Thank you Lord that in every situation, You are with me. Even in this!!

Oscar – A Widow's Friend

Oscar was a friend, true and faithful. No fanfare or desire for notoriety or attention. He just wanted to do his part for his church family and the Lord. From what I hear, when Oscar found his way to God, the change was obvious.

Tom and I didn't know Oscar before he began his faith journey. But we were blessed to know him and call him a friend since that journey began. Tom and Oscar could stand around after church and talk forever about anything. That was their way. Oscar always had a smile and a handshake for me and a high five for my five year old grandson, Tony. Tony loved Oscar and always needed to find him before we left church to go home. Usually on Sundays, Oscar was in the front foyer, visiting with people with that bright smile of his, so saying our goodbyes was easy. But a few times, usually on Wednesday night, he would be busy, turning off lights or securing the doors of the church. He was very conscientious about those things. On those occasions, we would wait in the front or walk around the building to find him. If Tony saw his truck outside, then we had to search for him to say our goodbyes, give hugs and give that high five to His big buddy.

After Tom died in October of 2013, Oscar took it upon himself to make sure my mower was up and running. I had mentioned to him, in passing, that I was having some issues with it. So he decided to drop by and take a look at it. He even brought his trailer so if he needed to take it home to work on it, he could. And that ended up happening a couple of times. On one occassion, when he brought it back, he decided to test it and mowed my yard for me, the whole yard. Tony was thrilled when Oscar came by the house, because he could stand outside and talk to him, watching him as he worked on this or that. There was one time when Tony told him about the mower not working just so he would stop by the house. It was such a sweet relationship, especially after Tom went to heaven. Oscar filled a gap in little Tony's life when his Wowo died. And now that Oscar has gone on to glory, he will be greatly missed by my grandson and me.

Oscar also proved to be a special blessing to my 80 year old aunt when she came to our church for a visit a few years ago. He went out of his way to walk outside and escort her into the church. I believe that she was having a little trouble walking that day because of some hip pain. He saw it as she crossed the street and went outside, took her arm, sharing that special smile of his, and led her inside. She was very impressed by his courteous and kind action, mentioning it to me several times over the following months. She would ask me how he was doing and if he treated all the ladies that way. I told her that, he did indeed, treat many ladies with the same chivalrous thoughtfulness.

Oscar loved the music of the church. Many times on Wednesday nights, as I led worship from the piano, I would see him standing at the back clapping his hands, singing, and a few times doing a little dance. He especially loved some of the hymns such as 'I have decided to follow Jesus', 'Just as I am', 'Victory in Jesus', 'How great Thou art' and several others. He also enjoyed the music on Sundays and would sincerely and with heartfelt devotion, enter in. It was so precious to see his love for the Lord and the sincerity that he displayed in his worship.

One particular Wednesday night, Tony and I arrived early in preparation for the worship service. I had been working with Tony, teaching him to sing 'Jesus Loves Me'. On this night, Oscar was also there early, turning on the lights and opening up the building. Tony decided to sing his new song for Oscar. So I sat at the piano to play and Tony grabbed a microphone to sing, the song he called 'Bible Jesus'. Oscar stood down front listening intently and when Tony was done he clapped enthusiastically as though it was the best performance he had ever heard. Tony beamed from his praise. It was a very special moment for both of them.

Dear Oscar, we will truly miss you. You are such a kind-hearted and caring man. Thank you for your friendship and for loving Tony through one of the most difficult times of his young life, the loss of his grandpa. I know that you are probably already visiting with my Tom and sharing all about what's been going on in our lives down here. The saying is so true, "Our loss is definitely heaven's gain."

Alone!! 6-3-15

Alone, so alone. How do I deal with this intense pain and loss. My Tom loved me best. He loved me completely. Other than the Lord, I was number one in his life and he was number one in mine. Now I'm so alone! I feel like no one would really miss me if I died. I know that my kids and grandkids love me. I know that a part of them would miss me but they have their own families and would get over my loss quickly. I know people at church, my friends that I sing with, my siblings and extended family love me and would miss me for a while but not for long. They also would go on with their lives, as they should.

But how do I go on with my life without Tom. He was so much a part of who I am. I could talk to him about anything and he would understand and not judge. Now I'm floundering, adrift in a vast sea of grief. I pray and read my Bible. I quote scriptures and wait on the Lord. I rebuke vain imaginations and the depression that pushes me down in Jesus name. And yet, I still feel so alone and abandoned. I am NOT abandoned but I feel that way. The Lord is always near and holds me close. He provides for me constantly in so many ways. I'm in such a battle!

I want to be strong and full of faith. I don't want to have these feelings where I just want to curl up in a ball in the back of my closet. What will I do when the kids move out? How will I cope with a house totally quiet? Somehow I must find a way to consistently stay on top of my grief. I cannot allow it to drag me under these tumultuous waves of sorrow and loneliness.

My friends would be surprised by my weakness. Everyone thinks that I am so strong. But I'm not! I'm hanging on for dear life because I want to please the Lord. I don't want to let people down who look up to me. I don't want to cause anyone to stumble or doubt. I don't want to give in to the weights that will drag me under. I desire the plan and future that God has for me to come forth. I must be used by God to make an eternal difference in people's lives.

Oh Lord most high, I put my trust in You. You alone can bring me through this dark valley of despair. You alone can be my strength when I am so weak. You alone see my true heart and know my thoughts.

I choose You, oh Lord. Even if no other stands with me or sees my true intentions and motives, I know that You do. Tom stood by me for 40 years. Help me to remember that You have stood by me for all of my years and will throughout eternity. Thank you Lord!! Help me to keep my eyes on You and not look for the approval and validation of other people.

Look deep into my heart, and cleanse me if there is anything there that shouldn't be there. Help me to see it so I can repent of it and allow You to remove it and make me into the woman You want me to be.

I surrender to You Oh Lord most High! Thy will be done! Your name be glorified!

A Widow's Journey 10-6-15

October 6, 2013 will remain a day that changed everything for me. That was the day that my dear husband of forty years was promoted to Glory. I truly expected for us to have, perhaps a dozen or so, more years together. We were both dealing with health issues that come with age, but were facing them together and working through those things with the Lord's help.

During the two years since Tom's death, I have learned so much. My sensitivity to those around me has been heightened. I see the struggles that they are going through and want to help. But I also realize that I am and have been truly blessed throughout my life. Even now, although dealing with waves of grief and loneliness at times, I see how God's hand is upon me and that HE walks with me. What a blessing to know Him in this way, to have that assurance that I am never alone. And if I will allow Him to, He will lead and even intervene in each situation. If I could permit those hurting and careworn people around me to get a glimpse of Him through my eyes, I would. But they must seek and find Him for themselves. So I do what I can with the abilities and talents that God has given to me, to communicate His great love and faithfulness.

God has opened many new doors for me. Singing at my local church, Brazoria 1st Assembly and with my friends in Appointed by Grace, has allowed me the opportunity to share my experiences and God's goodness through music for many years. But the Lord has opened other doors as well, leading me to communicate not only in song but through His Word and with stories. I had felt an urging from the Lord to begin writing down our stories several years ago. And then after Tom's death, I felt God's nudge to share these stories with others online. This was not easy since I am a very private person. When I began to speak, more than a year ago, I didn't really see how He could use me in this way. But He has, helping me to overcome the nervousness and insecurity of public speaking that had always come naturally to my husband but not to me.

As I went to my devotion, dated October 6, I found again the Lord's assurance and affirmation in the direction of my journey. Although on that date, it seemed like I had come to the end of my life, my precious God and Friend has turned it around into something new and beautiful.

Over and over again, whether directly from His Word or due to people that He has inspired through other words or writings, He continues to validate, encourage and inspire me to keep moving forward on this road He's leading me down. What a privilege to be used by God to make a positive and eternal difference in someone's life. If you like something I write or enjoy listening to me sing, Praise God! All the glory goes to Him! I couldn't do any of it without Him. He made this instrument, named Vonnie, with her own unique abilities. It's my responsibility to develop those talents, to stay close to Him and in His Word so I don't get off track and to keep this vessel clean and ready for Him to use and flow through without hindrance.

But guess what!! God doesn't play favorites. He wants to use you also!! AWESOME, RIGHT?!!

Memories of the Man That I Love 12-15-15

The man that I love brought me flowers, maybe even a card,
Sometimes beautiful roses, at times buds from the yard.

The man that I love liked his football, stomped his feet and yelled at
the screen
Rejoiced when there was a victory, made excuses for his losing team.

The man that I love was so funny, he bellowed with laughter and glee
When he shared corny jokes with the family, then lovingly grinned
at me.

The man that I love was amazing, was a plumber, electrician and more.
He could do anything, build a shelf, fix a car, but couldn't find spices
at the store.

The man that I love was not perfect, he was always leaving a mess
But thank God he was there to make them, for that I am truly blessed.

The man that I love made decisions, ones that I didn't want to face.
He always asked for my input, then decided and bore under the weight.

The man that I love was most tender, tearing up at a mountainous scene
Choking back muffled sobs at the sadness, losing a loved-one can bring.

The man that I love was demanding, giving orders to complete a task.
Bring me this, get me that was his query, then it's fixed and holding fast.

The man that I love gave me cuddles, held me gently as he kissed me
Oh, what sweet, tender moments, for it is in his embrace, I'm complete.

The man that I love adores music, got shivers when my singing was
fine,
was always there to encourage, always making me feel like I shine.

Be thankful for your man God's provided, with his ups and his downs
and his fears,

Keep him close, let him know you respect him, tell him often you hold him most dear.
Be patient when he is not perfect, understanding when he is not clear,
For if you're able to wake up beside him, you are blessed to have him so near.

Reflections From God's Heart

A Cut Above

When a professional jeweler prepares to cut a precious stone such as a diamond, ruby, emerald or sapphire, he doesn't just start whittling away. There is not, a wait-and-see attitude, as to what it will be. He studies the jewel thoughtfully, exposing it with the proper lighting, so he can carefully consider it from every side and angle. And then, as he expectantly lays out his intricate tools, he plans the shape, size and purpose for the stone. Will it be a brilliant solitaire in a ring? Will it end up as several smaller, dazzling crystals that are made into a bracelet, earrings or pendant? You see, this is a precious stone, one of tremendous value. He knows exactly the cuts that he will make before he handles the chisel. They are planned according to the purpose of the piece. The cuts are not given carelessly or haphazardly, but thoughtfully and precisely. If the stone could reason, it might not understand all of the cuts that are so cautiously made. It might wonder at the heat that is being applied or the delay because of the lengthy preparation. The jewel might be anxious to realize its purpose and to be admired by its new owner. However, the jeweler does understand the process and the delays. He knows the setting, its strengths and its weaknesses. He is the master jeweler and knows right where the stone will best fit and shine its very brightest.

So it is with us, God's greatest and most precious creation. He carefully plans each procedure and cut in preparation for our ultimate purpose and setting. He knows the timing, temperature and the precision that are needed. Our plan will be our very own, not the same as any other. We are unique and have been created for a function designed just for us. Will we be patient through the process, when we don't understand why things happen the way they do? Can we keep our eyes on the Master Designer, when He leads us in a direction that seems contrary to the plan? Will we stand firm and still when the temperatures of life seem too intense? Do we trust Him through the delays, even when it appears to be taking much too long? Unlike the precious stone, we have a choice in the final determination of our purpose. If we will patiently keep our focus on the Lord and trust in Him, then we will find that joy of fulfillment, realizing His eternal plan and achieving His will in our lives. And through this faith-filled surrender to His loving and tender hands, each one of us will be made A CUT ABOVE.

Isaiah 40:31

"Those that wait upon the Lord, shall renew their strength,
they shall mount up with wings as eagles. They shall run
and not grow weary, they shall walk and not faint."

I have known and served the Lord all my life. From an infant, I was raised in church, had parents who taught and disciplined God's way. I learned all the Bible stories, memorized the scriptures, and prayed earnestly and fervently. I have seen many miracles and have questioned some of God's answers. But knowing Him intimately has helped me to deal with those times when the ways of God were unclear and seemingly silent. He is a loving and powerful God, not surprised or daunted by any situation or circumstance. He is still able to handle each one. We must work on OUR perspective.

Even after all of my history with the Lord, sometimes situations (the winds, waves, storms of life, etc.) can cause me to take my eyes off of Him and forget, momentarily, what an awesome and loving friend He is. Again, I am reminded that I must stay close to my Lord, keep my eyes on Him, and not be distracted by others and those voices that try to bring fear and doubts into my life.

When we **wait upon** the Lord (hope in, look to, remember who he is) our **strength is renewed**. We're given new strength and endurance.

We soar - gain new perspective – see things more clearly –
We are able to see more of the whole picture through Him.

We run and not grow weary - we store up extra energy.

We walk and faint not - we deepen our determination to persevere. We gain strength from the Lord and receive insight from His Word.

We find understanding and remembrance from friends and family in the Lord. They remind us of God's greatness and love.

They help restore proper vision through His Word and their testimonies. And once again, we remember that He is our strength and help in every season of life. So, let us wait upon the Lord!

A Life Lived Effectively

I just finished watching one of my favorite holiday movies, "It's a Wonderful Life". Again, I was drawn into the story of a man, George Bailey, who unknowingly and yet positively affected many lives around him. While facing his own set of circumstances in life, its disappointments and setbacks, he continued to help others and make a difference, for the good of his family, friends and community. And again I cried at the end when all of the people that he had helped in his life, rallied around to help him out of dire circumstances, not of his own making.

I love this movie for many reasons. One reason is that I get to have a good cry from it, one that brings happy tears and a smile to my face. Another reason is that it's a reminder of the affect we each have on the people around us every day, whether good or bad. We don't usually approach each day thinking about who we might help. We just live life, not knowing how our words and deeds will impact others. Those seemingly insignificant actions just seem to happen as a common, everyday occurrence without us realizing the depth and importance of them. It appears that we aren't really accomplishing anything and yet through all of the small things we ARE making a difference.

This movie also causes me to reflect on all of those people in my own life who through the years, have helped shape me into the person I am today.

My parents top the list because they introduced me to Jesus and His people. That's where my main foundation was firmly laid. I'm so thankful, that from the beginning, I was taught about the Lord. In my family, church was a mainstay of life, not just an occasional addition. Even through the really hard times of separation and divorce, my mom kept me in church. Although working full time, she still made sure I was involved in every youth group and school activity. My dad introduced me to a loving heavenly Father, through his words and by his example of being an adoring father. Even though our time together was limited, after my parent's divorce when I was nine, Dad made good use of our time to teach me the things of God. And even though I was not of her blood, my second mom, Betty, always treated me like a daughter and loved me as a mom should. I had three prime examples of the love of God while growing up.

Others who impacted my life were my Pastors down through the years: the Nashes and Jacksons; the Bascoms and Shenemans; the Redfearns, Flowers and Frankums. All of these men and women of God showed me Jesus with skin on and their teachings and love made all of the difference.

Then there were the teachers – school teachers, choir, Sunday school and Bible teachers. Also, my piano and voice teachers, Gertrude and Nell Mann. Their wealth of wisdom and knowledge was of tremendous value. But even more than that, was the encouragement to excel, dream and pursue those dreams. I've always tried to follow in their footsteps, giving to those around me also. I've tried to speak positive, encouraging and faith-building words.

Have there been those who have tried to squelch and diminish my giftings and God's calling on my life? Have there been the Mr. Potters, like with George Bailey, just waiting and hoping that one day I would fall down or give up? Sure there have. Sometimes they did it on purpose and sometimes without realizing what they were doing. It's our choice to hold on to our dreams and the calling that God has placed on our life. We must find that purpose and plan that He has for each and every one of us and pursue it. I wonder if any of these encouragers realize the impact they had on my life alone, as well as all the others individuals that they touched, down through the years.

So what's the conclusion to all of this contemplation? We each make a tremendous difference in the lives of the people around us. Their existence would not be as rich and full if it were not for your input and effect on them. So don't ever think that somehow you don't matter or that what you do is not important. That's just not true. Constantly, every day, through small and seemingly insignificant words and deeds, we bring life and hope into the lives of other people.

When Jesus is in control of our life, ours… and theirs… can be a wonderful life.

Psalm 27

*"I am still confident of this, I will see the goodness of
the Lord in the land of the living." Psalm 27:13*
I am still confident, despite all I see.
I am still assured, despite all I hear.
I am still resolved, despite all I feel.
I will wait for Him patiently.
I will seek after Him expectantly.
I will work for Him tirelessly.
I will stand strong without wavering.
I will take heart and trust courageously
For His timing is perfect and His will is complete.
The Lord heals to restore us to the purpose
for which we were born.

All are Needed

We are all a vitally important part of the Kingdom of God. Each person, both young and old, can have great impact upon those around them when following God's design and plan. We each have our own unique talent and we are needed.

Young people think, "I am so young, just a teenager, who will listen to me, what can I do?" They don't think that they can make a difference. But God has used 'just teens or youths' for great exploits before.

Many older people think "My time is past, how can God use me?" Somehow we need to realize that God doesn't just speak through middle aged adults. He will use all of us, if we are determined to be available and to be led by Him. The Lord can move through those who are faithful, dependable and who want to truly know Him.

The Word of God is full of examples of young and old, who were used mightily by God. Who are some of these teenagers and elders?

There's David, who was a simple shepherd but who loved God and stayed close to Him in his early years. He defeated a giant and became a great leader and King. Then there's Esther, who was an orphaned young woman, being raised by an uncle while living in exile in a foreign country. She became queen and saved a whole race of people from genocide because of her character and devotion to God.

Young Joseph was sold into slavery by his own brothers, falsely accused and thrown into prison. And yet, because he faithfully trusted and served God through it all, over the course of thirteen years, he became second in command over all of Egypt.

Consider Moses, who at the age of 80 obediently followed God's voice and delivered the entire nation of Israel out of cruel slavery.

And Noah, who was well advanced in years but stood firm in his beliefs and faithfulness to God to save humanity.

Bear in mind, Abraham, who diligently followed and trusted God's leading to a new land he knew nothing about and then established an eternal covenant.

There are other examples also. All of these were called to service and because of their faith and devotion to God, they did impressive things for their people and God's Kingdom. They didn't allow the world around them to influence their decisions. Satan tried to deceive them and to destroy them in various ways because he knows the power of a committed person, no matter the age. Awesome Power!!

This world and the enemy will try to pull us down and draw us away from our future in God. Let's NOT allow it! Let's realize now that we are an amazing force, through Christ and for the Kingdom of God (Satan knows it!). Let's not follow the crowd and live a ho-hum, average existence, like most of the world. Let's follow Jesus and live a life of excellence, excitement, fulfillment and fellowship with God.

God's way is not the way of the world. People don't realize this. They think that they can just float along with the crowd on the outside edges of grace and still live a life that's pleasing and obedient to God. Some people call that walking on the fence, but God calls it being lukewarm. And we know what He said about THAT! It makes Him sick.

Most of the time, going God's way will mean going upstream against the flow and the crowd. It can be a totally different direction and sometimes we have to fight against the current. But if we are committed and stay close to the Savior, the current doesn't affect us, because He is leading the way through. And when we follow closely to Him, we are in His wake and the going is easier. It's when we stray too far away from the Lord, trying to do it 'our way' that the going gets really rough. When we try to fit into the world's way and God's way both, that's when we find that serving Him is so hard.

So, let's stay close to Jesus.

Let's determine to follow HIS path!

Let's choose to be obedient to His Way and His Word!

Let's seek Him daily!

Then, we will find that awesome life that He's planned for each and every one of us, whether young or old. Then, we WILL have a mighty and powerful impact on those around us, for God's kingdom and for eternity.

Faith

Faith is knowing something to be true in your heart, before you actually see it with your eyes. Will our worship depend upon what we see with our natural eyes or by what we see by faith with our spiritual eyes?

Will we wait for faith to become tangible and touchable before we offer our sincere and passionate praise to our Lord and King?

Let us give Him our praise now.

Let us see with spiritual eyes.

Be aware that our God is faithful and true.

He has promised great things to happen.

Can He trust us, to trust Him, through those times when we don't see the answer yet? That is faith.

Let us celebrate our God.

Let us celebrate His love, mercy and grace.

Let us celebrate His faithfulness.

He is worthy of all of our worship.

And let us do it now before the answer comes.

Faith pleases our God.

Prayer - Called to Righteousness

Purify my heart, oh Lord and I will be clean.
Create in me a clean heart.
Burn off all the dross of pride and selfishness.
Sweep away the cobwebs of doubt and fear that linger in the corners of my mind.
Sear away all the cynicism and sarcasm that like to inch their way into my attitude.
Flood me with the water of Your Holy Word till I am cleansed and sparkle.
Pour over me a fresh anointing of Your Holy Spirit to coat every crevice and area.
Then I will be a pure vessel ready for Your use, primed for the flow of Your Presence.
I love you Lord. I love being near You and doing Your will.
Use this servant as You see fit.
Move through me and in me. Form and mold me.
Change me as is needed to best suit YOUR plan to touch others.
Flow through me.

The Promises of God

The promises of God are not automatic, they must be established.
God's Word is already established in Heaven but must
also be established on earth. The promises of God are
confirmed through reading, speaking and believing
those promises. Don't live with a crushed spirit,
move past it by faith and through faith-
filled Words, spoken out loud.

Call those things that are not, as though they were.
Because through God, THEY ARE!

We Were Planned For God's Pleasure

"God takes pleasure in His people" Psalm 149:4

God is pleased when we spend time with Him and worship Him sincerely. The secret to a lifestyle of worship, is doing everything as if you are doing it for Jesus. Take your everyday, ordinary life – sleeping, eating, working, playing and walking around life – and place it before God as an offering. True worship is sincere and passionate, not formal and half-hearted.

If you find yourself going through the motions rather than giving God your focus, determine that you will change. Worshipping in spirit and in truth is an awesome experience that no one wants to miss out on. It ushers us into a realm of glory that many in this world have never known. And most of all, it brings a smile to God's face.

Loving Jesus is talking to Him throughout your day and thinking of Him in the same way you did when you were newly in love with your spouse. You and I were created to bring God pleasure and some of the many benefits of that are his amazing blessings, His favor, being part of an awesome family, and an incredible inheritance.

Make it one of your daily goals in life, to bring pleasure to God.

Great Things For God (Once in a lifetime?)

In today's society, we are challenged to do "Great Things". We are urged to excel and achieve, no matter what we must do to accomplish this. We are expected to climb to the top, even if that means pushing down or stepping on other people.

Of course, we as God's people know that the Lord does lead some of us to great deeds and important destinies. And we must be open to His plan and prepared if that is the case. We also know that if public greatness is the direction that God is leading us, it is because HE can trust us with it and HE will be the One to promote us. God will be the One to open and close doors according to His plan. All we must do is to know His voice and to be obedient to step forward at the right time.

For most of us, God has a plan of great importance to eternity but one that probably won't receive much notoriety or recognition. Whichever destiny is ours, there remains a constant. We must be faithful, each day, in the little things of life.

Small opportunities surround us, like telling the truth, being kind, generous, faithful, honest, trustworthy, forgiving and encouraging. We need to learn to hear and know God's voice. We must be quick to act in obedience. Then when the time comes for the Lord to use us, we will be prepared and ready. God is more pleased when we do the everyday small things for Him, out of loving devotion. They are actions and deeds that others don't see, but God does. All these things bring a smile to His face. You can't have the 'once in a lifetime' great things of God, without the small daily things!

Joseph, Esther and David are Biblical examples of people who had to learn daily, obedient devotion to God before they were ready to step into His Sovereign design for their lives. So whether our destiny in God leads to recognized greatness or hidden greatness, we need to learn to constantly stay close to Him, listening for His voice and walking in the way He opens before us. God treasures simple acts of obedience more than our prayers, praise and offerings. All are important, but obedience must come first. Then He is free to use the gifts and talents that He created in us, for His Eternal Kingdom and Glory!

Isaiah 53

Jesus was despised and rejected. He was a man familiar with sorrow and suffering. Did He start being despised when His ministry began? No, I don't believe so. His whole life was one of meekness, goodness and Godliness. He grew up in a small town, learning to work in the trade of carpentry. He was part of a family of humble origins and simple lifestyle. He was familiar with rejection, pain and loss, including the death of his earthly father, Joseph. He was tested in every area of life, according to the Word, and yet He didn't sin.

Jesus was highly intelligent and well-versed in Scripture. He amazed teachers and scholars, at the age of twelve, with His questions and knowledge. He was all man and yet He was also all God. I find it amazing that through Christ's questioning, beating, torture, suffering and crucifixion, Jesus offered no defense. The word says, "He spoke not a word". I'm reminded of an old song that goes like this:

"When a storm comes my way and I've had a bad day and my spirit has fallen so low, I feel so ashamed to have ever complained, when Jesus spoke not a word.

Oppressed and afflicted, no complaint did He make when His body was broken for me. A lamb to the slaughter, despised and rejected, yet my Jesus spoke not a word.

We have all gone astray and have turned our own way, and upon Him was laid our sin, yet in the trials He went through for me and for you, my Jesus spoke not a word."

Here was a Man of verbal excellence, able to hold thousands spellbound with His stories, wisdom and insight. Here was a Man whom scholars and teachers marveled at, when He shared His knowledge and discernment. And yet, Jesus chose not to speak up for Himself. Why? Why would He do that? Because, He CHOSE to go through the rejection and He CHOSE to endure the horrible, relentless beatings. He CHOSE to tolerate ridicule and mockery and He CHOSE to pay the supreme price of an excruciating death on the cross for our sins, our mistakes and our failings.

WHAT AN INCREDIBLE LOVE!!

Delayed Not Denied

Sometimes in life we experience delays that feel like and give the strong appearance of denial. We think that because the answer doesn't come "right now" that God must not be listening or that He's just saying "no". However, we also know that many things in life DO take time and can't be rushed.

When told that we are expecting a precious baby, do we look at the Doctor and say, "But I don't want to wait all those months, can't we do this now?" No, of course not. We understand and comprehend that all those months provide time for the growth and development of that unique little person. But also, it gives a time for planning and preparation for the mommy and daddy. It gives time for them to get ready emotionally, mentally, physically and spiritually. And there's time for that special bond to grow between the parents and the baby.

We don't question the delay in this situation because we understand and trust the need for it. Isn't that how it should be with the other areas in our life, especially the ones where we've prayed and are relying on our Heavenly Father for the answer? I know, I know, it's harder in those cases. I struggle with this also. We don't have the same outlook and understanding. It doesn't make sense. But we CAN have the same trust and realization that this delay, could be a necessary thing.

Again, it's a matter of OUR perspective. We must stay close to and in touch with the ONE with the answers, the ONE who loves us enough to die for us. I know for myself, that sometimes, life can seem hard and unfair. But I have found from personal experience that staying close to the Lord through prayer, His Word and through His people is invaluable. Learning His promises, reading them and speaking them out loud makes a world of difference in MY outlook. Those delays in life become more bearable and make a little more sense.

They become delays rather than denials.

Knowing Him: Lord, You Are....

Who is this God that we serve and follow? What do we comprehend about Him?

Do we really know Him or just about Him? Are we seeking to experience Him personally? Would knowing Him intimately help us to live more effective, useful and happy lives? What does His Word say?

*Matthew 7:21-23 "Not everyone who says to me, 'Lord, Lord,' will enter the kingdom of heaven, but only he who does the will of my Father who is in Heaven. Many will say on that day, 'Lord, Lord, did we not prophesy in Your name, and in Your name drive out demons and perform many miracles? Then I will tell them plainly, **I never knew you**, Away from me, you evil doers!'*

The fact that our criteria for entering into heaven depends on truly knowing the Lord and not just having knowledge about Him and doing works for Him, should spur us into seeking after Him, to gaining discernment of Him and to spending time with Him. Does this revelation of His desire for us to know Him make prophesying, driving out demons and performing miracles wrong? Of course not!!

It does give us direction for our priorities, though. Again, what does the Word say? *Mark 12: 29-31 "The most important one (commandment)", Jesus answered, "is this: 'Hear Oh Israel, the Lord our God, the Lord is One. Love the Lord your God with all of your heart, with all of your soul, with all of your mind and with all of your strength. The second is this, Love your neighbor as yourself. There is no commandment greater than these."*

KNOW GOD and love Him how? With all of our heart, soul, mind and strength.

In other words, we are to know Him with all that is within us, with every fiber of our being. Each of us, individually, must seek after the Lord to know Him in our own way and in our own capacity. We are all at different levels of maturity in the Lord. We all progress at different paces and various speeds. So join me in this journey to know Him. I will share my limited knowledge and you are welcome to share yours. And together we will learn to know Him. And then let's take that knowledge and do those things that He has called each of us to do.

Lord, You are... my new beginning. I choose to know You each and every day. I choose to know about You through Your Word and through Your people. I choose to know You by spending time with You in my quiet moments and throughout my day. Lord, You are... my catalyst. Hearing is easy, doing is hard.

But I can do all things through You who strengthens me.

It takes thoughtful, deliberate action to be a doer of the Word and not a hearer only.

It doesn't just happen when circumstances are right. Many times, planning is necessary. I choose to listen for Your voice and to obey Your voice.

I choose to KNOW YOU!!

Isaiah 58

"IF you keep your feet from breaking the Sabbath and from doing as <u>YOU</u>
please on
<u>MY</u> *holy day, IF you call the Sabbath a delight and the Lord's day honorable and*
<u>IF</u> *you honor it by not going* <u>YOUR</u> *own way and doing as* <u>YOU</u> *please, or speaking idle* (thoughtless, silly, meaningless, selfish) *words.....*

<u>THEN</u>, *YOU will find your joy* (peaceful, bubbling happiness) *in the Lord, and I will cause YOU to ride on the heights of the land* (existing above circumstance, able to deal successfully with each days challenges) *and to feast* (joyfully partake of abundance) *on the inheritance of your father Jacob.* (who received blessings, favor, esteem and honor from his father and from his Lord). *The mouth of the Lord has spoken.* (This is a promise, firm and sure, ready for the taking.) *Isaiah 58:13, 14*

I have always known that it was important to observe and honor the Lord on the Sabbath. I have tried to do this all my life and have for the most part. There was a time in my younger years when it was necessary to work on some Sundays.

Sundays have always been my Sabbath, a day set aside to honor the Lord, learn more of Him, and fellowship with other believers as we seek to know Him together. If your day is Saturday, that's fine. I don't think the Lord minds what day of the week we choose, as long as there is a day set aside for Him.

But guess what... The Lord doesn't zap us or slap us upside the head if we don't keep the Sabbath. It's our choice. There are always consequences. But ultimately, we are the ones choosing to 'receive the blessings that accompany the obedience' or choosing to 'forfeit those blessings by GOING OUR OWN WAY'. God will not force His blessings on us, but they are there for us to enjoy if WE choose. The blessing is a result of the obedience, just like the intake of vitamin C is the result from eating an orange. Here's one other thought. If observing, honoring and delighting in the Sabbath brings such blessings and benefit into our lives, what would spending some time giving our full attention to the Lord every day do? Think on it.

Everyday Blessings

It takes a dry, still, breathless, sun-scorched day, where the heat rises up in visible waves, to cause us to appreciate the small, everyday blessings that we would normally take for granted.

Blessings like:

Big fluffy clouds, that give a momentary break from the sun.
A lightly blowing breeze, that turns the sweat on your brow into a cool touch.
An unexpected summer shower, that brings refreshing but also the sweetest aroma that we breathe in deeply with a sense of joy.
A cold glass of iced tea or lemonade, that quenches the deepest thirst.
Sitting under a beautiful, large shade tree, that seems to cause the day to cool by several degrees.
The cool spray from a waterfall or fountain, that brings a sigh of relief.
Wading through a crystal clear stream, splashing the cool water over arms and legs and enjoying it so much that you don't even care if you get wet.
The dry, difficult and quiet times in life, can cause us to reflect back on these small blessings. We learn to appreciate those refreshing moments that God provides for us every day. His blessings are endless and His mercies are new every morning.

Hosea Betroths Gomer

God, the Almighty One, is the Creator of everything. He is all powerful, all knowing, all encompassing and wants to be our Beloved, our Husband and our Friend. What an incredible thought! The depth of such a love as His, is beyond our understanding. That is why God wanted the prophet Hosea to emulate and set the example of such devotion, as a revelation of His great love for us. It was to be a life lesson that most people would question and behold in shocked unbelief.

Hosea said "I will betroth you to me forever." In a betrothal, the bride is pure, sweet and innocent. The groom looks at her through love-filled, reality-clouded eyes. Her flaws and imperfections are not evident but are hidden from view. His bride is perfect, unlike any other woman, untouched and waiting just for him.

God called Hosea to betroth Gomer like a new bride, although she was far from pure, righteous or innocent. She had known the sincere love of her husband, Hosea. She had born him children, living within the covenant and committed life of a wife and mother. And yet she turned from him, rejected his provision, his love, his protection and his friendship. She turned from a life of righteousness and honor to one of prostitution and bondage.

Although rejected and reviled, Hosea bought her back at a tremendous expense to his pride and bank account. She had placed herself in a position of utter failure, deep shame and desperation. She was totally lost without a glimmer of hope or expectation for redemption and restoration. And yet her husband, at God's command and to reveal His depth of love for us, bought her back.

He redeemed her and forgave her.

Then again, he betrothed her – looking at her through groom's eyes, seeing her as untouched, pure and beautiful!!

What an awesome, unsearchable and unfathomable sacrifice!!

What an incredible insight into God's forgiveness and incomprehensible love for us!

Is The Easy Way God's Way?

God has called us to live an overcoming life, full of joy, peace and love. Does that mean that we should seclude ourselves somewhere away from people? Because let's face it, people can make achieving that daily walk of victory, very difficult. There are preachers out there that encourage their people to avoid contact with those who will bring them down... to not associate with others who might discourage them or cause them to stumble... and to be careful not to trust everyone or to confide in them. I agree with this to a certain extent. Wisdom and Godly discernment is required in our everyday dealings with our fellow man.

But, what did Jesus do as an example to us? Did He associate with people of questionable character? Yes. Did he reach out and try to build bridges to those who spoke against Him? Yes. Did He forgive and try to encourage those closest to Him when they betrayed Him or slept when He needed them to pray? Yes.

So why do we turn down a different aisle at the store when we see someone that we've had a disagreement with in the past? That's the easy way. Is the easy way, Gods way? Let's try letting go of it, saying hello and maybe even hugging their neck instead. Wow, could healing flow from that? Maybe.

How about inviting that relative that gets on everybody's nerves to the next family function? Just maybe, they need some encouragement. I know that I ask a hard thing. It's so much easier to just, accidentally, forget to invite them and be assured an evening of peace and fun. But is the easy way God's way?

What about that person, whom you trusted, that betrayed you and practically destroyed your life in the past. Should an effort be made to restore that relationship? Should you take the chance of being hurt or offended again. It's so much easier to just ignore their existence. "I'll go my way, they can go their way." But is the easy way God's way? I don't think so. And no matter how many excuses you come up with, deep down, as a disciple and follower of Christ, you know the answer to these questions.

Relationships are precious and shouldn't be shoved aside because of hurt, betrayal or disagreements. God wants friends and families to be restored and healed. We must be genuinely free to live that overcoming life of victory.

Let's TRULY forgive and go the extra mile and work toward restoration. Everyone knows that there are exceptions, especially when someone is dangerous or involved in addictions. In that case, forgive and keep your distance, until it's safe. But those cases are not what I'm talking about here. Use Godly wisdom and discernment. Let's try to consistently go God's way, although it may be a bit harder. Let's face it, Jesus told us that in this life there WOULD be trouble. But we know that it will be okay and we can keep our joy because He has overcome the world. His way works. Things like healing, forgiveness and restoration don't usually come easily, but they are worth the effort and the cost. And they ARE God's way!

II Chronicles 7:14

"If My people, who are called by My name, shall humble themselves and pray and seek My face and turn from their wicked ways; then will I hear from heaven and will forgive their sin and will heal their land." II Chronicles 7:14

"If My people who are called by My name" - we who belong to the Lord and claim to be His
"Shall humble themselves and pray" - put aside pride and prestige, admit our need for our Lord
"And seek My face and turn from their wicked ways" - to search out the Lord and to purposely turn to what is right

THEN *I will hear from heaven* - He is aware and gives clear direction

I will forgive their sin - He gives restoration, grace and mercy *I will heal their land* - we will receive God's favor, promises and glory When God's face looks our way, we have His favor!! When we seek diligently for Him, He responds!!

When a small child really wants the attention of a parent, what does she do? She comes skipping and dancing around the parent, calling out to him. The adult may be on the phone, talking to a friend or busy on some task. Does the child quit? Not if she really wants them to notice and listen to her. She keeps on, and if necessary, will pull on her parent's clothes. She continually calls out "Mama" or "Papa" until their face turns toward her.

Sometimes, we as parents don't always give our full attention. We will try to placate the child or send her on a task so we can get back to what we're doing. God isn't like that. Once we get His attention (by seeking Him), we find His favor.

Have you ever seen a child climb onto a grown-ups lap and grab both sides of their face, so the adult is looking her in the eye? She is "seeking his face" isn't she? Are we hungry enough for God's attention and favor that we don't give up with the skipping and dancing? Do we move on to the tugging and pulling or even

continue to "seek His face" by climbing onto His lap and g
His face to look us in the eye?

When God's face is turned our way, His favor is turned our way
(when we seek Him honestly and sincerely).

Now, God isn't like a parent who's distracted or busy. He doesn't
make us turn back flips for His attention and favor. But we must do
some seeking. We must show that we are truly wanting and desiring
His Presence and full attention. We need to take time to examine
ourselves, repent, purify our hearts, turn from ungodly ways and
truly seek His face. He's always ready to give us His full attention
for He loves us with a deep abiding love. His love is so much greater
than what we have for our own children.

But many times, we want His favor and face without any effort.
We want the glory, blessing and favor of God without the repentance
and seeking. But God is good and patient and sometimes He gives
us His support anyway. Sometimes He shows us glimpses of His
glory. But are we content with glimpses? That's like being satisfied
with the crumbs from a banquet table. I don't want just crumbs. I
want all that God has prepared for me at this banquet feast. Are
we willing to pursue God to gain His favor and dwell in His glory?

Many times we are like a teenager, who wants the parent's
attention, calling from the other room, wanting the adult to come
to him. If the teen really wants that parent, he will go to them. Yes,
many times God shows up when we call. But the Word tells US to
seek HIS face. We are to go TO HIM, and then we will find a new
depth of love and favor. Think about it. When are you touched most
by your child? When she calls you to come to her in another room to
ask for something, or when she searches the house for you, climbs
onto your lap, grabs your face, looks into your eyes and says, "I love
you"? When is your favor the strongest toward that child? When does
your heart melt with love? Aren't we made in God's image? Don't we
have His Son living in us? Then mustn't God feel similar? Wouldn't
He be touched by our "Seeking of Him"? Do we love Him enough
to take time to seek Him or are we content to just call from the other
room, hoping that He comes? Why would we be content with crumbs
of His glory when we can have a feast and dwell in His presence?

The full attention and favor of God looking right at us - imagine
that.

What an awesome thought!!

"Win One For The Gipper"

You've heard the old saying, "Win one for the Gipper". You've seen the true stories about the football team that's struggling to prove their worth. They are on the verge of tremendous victory and something happens to their star player or coach. So they rally together with great determination and they dedicate that championship game to that special person. I love those stories of triumph in the abject face of defeat. I get to have one of my happy cries and go away from the movie with a feeling of contentment and euphoria.

As I opened my Bible this morning, I found a little slip of paper that I wrote and put in there back in September 2000. That's at the time when my precious dad went to heaven. While going through his Bible, my siblings and I found a similar piece of paper. On it was written these words "Is what Jim Patterson living for worth Jesus dying for?" I was so touched by the message and the charge for excellence, that I wrote those words with my own name inserted and placed it in my own Bible. It reminds me that each day of my life is an opportunity to live to the fullest and to "win one for the Gipper" or in my case to "win one for Jesus". And let's face it, as touching and inspiring as those moments are in life when we take on an impossible challenge in honor or memory of another, how much more is it to live each day with eternity in sight, touching and affecting the precious people for whom Jesus died.

Oh Lord, may each day that I live, honor the sacrifice that You made.

May I determine each new day to "win this one for Jesus".

A Springboard For Greatness

As I started out on this particular day, I went to one of my favorite sources of devotions. It's a 365 day prayer journal called "Prayers that Avail much". For each day of the year, there is a scripture prayer that addresses a subject or situation of life that we all deal with at one point or another. That is followed by the scripture references used in the prayer and, in my way of thinking, to be studied in more detail. Then there is a faith-filled daily confession, which I believe is more powerful and establishes the truth, if spoken out loud. And finally it ends with a few blank lines where you can write your own thoughts about what you learned and gleaned from the study.

Now on some days, I come away from my devotion time thinking "Hmm, that was interesting. Thank you Lord for that insight." But on many more days I come away from my devotion time thinking, "Wow Lord, that was an incredible look into Your heart, Your plan and Your care for me! Thank You!!" (As a side note, my 'Wow' days usually happen when I take more time with the Lord and I'm not so rushed.)

Today was a 'Wow' day.

As I looked at the date, January 23, I remembered that today would have been my Dad's 82nd birthday. As I reflected and reminisced about him and what he meant to my life, I wished him a 'Happy Birthday', wondering if they celebrate birthdays in heaven. Dad was a man who strove for excellence in every area of life, but especially in his relationship with the Lord. He was very smart, quite handsome and commanded respect from those he worked with. He was a leader and felt the weight of responsibility to correct or fix things and situations that weren't quite right.

Sometimes his A-type personality and the need to control conditions, got him into trouble. He was human and just like all of us, made mistakes. But he was also fun, silly, energetic and very loving. He was a great example to me and I was so blessed to call him Daddy. But in every area of life, whether playing with his children and grandchildren or commanding a unit of military men and women, he stood for and displayed Godly integrity.

I remember that dad had constructed a special prayer-closet for himself at one of the last houses in which he and mother lived in

Hendersonville, Tennessee. He proudly showed it to us when we came for a visit. It was his very own sanctuary or 'War Room', where he could get away from phones and paperwork and spend some quality time with the Lord.

As I studied the scripture reading today, I thought about how it related to my life but also how it related to my dad's life. I considered his humble beginnings as a boy on his family's farm in the small community of Iberia, Missouri. I pondered how he went on to graduate high school, then college and later on to achieve his Masters Degree at Tulane University. He served for 25+ years in the military and retired a Lieutenant Colonel, after serving one tour in Korea and two stints in Vietnam. Then he continued on, serving the Lord in the leadership of churches and of a well-known and beloved television ministry. At one point, he was the Financial Director for Pat Robertson's presidential campaign. Throughout his life, he held himself to a high and Godly standard and because of that faced persecution, rejection and some ridicule. I'm sure there were times when he blew it and wished he had handled a situation differently. We all go through that. But ultimately, he became a man who did great things for his country and mighty exploits for his God.

The phrase that caught my attention this special day was this. "Lord, You are able to use every circumstance of my life as a springboard for greatness." I thought about dad and all that he endured to achieve what the Lord had called him to. And I thought about myself and all of the places I've been, the people I've known and the experiences that I've had. I can look back now and see how many of these places, people and episodes impacted and changed me. They made me into the person that I needed to become, in order to fulfill God's plan and purpose for my life. Some of those seasons of life were very painful, but were also times that brought me closer to the Lord and thereby strengthened my resolve and faith.

As we obediently follow Christ, staying constant in His truth and ways, through the good and the difficult times of life, we will find our own level of greatness according to His plan and will. And because of that obedience and faithfulness, He is able to use every circumstance of our lives as a 'Springboard for greatness'.

The River (from a vision given by God in 1999)

I see a long and wide river, alive and sparkling with life and light. The light shines up from the depths of the river, illuminating the water and even the sky above. The water glows with a myriad of colors and is epervescent and vivid. Totally alive!! As you travel away from the river, there is darkness. But the closer you come to the water's edge there is light and life.

There are all kinds of people from every walk of life in that living river. Some are ankle deep, some are knee deep and others are in up to their waist. These stand there just soaking in the life while watching the activities in the deeper water. Then there are those out in the deeper waters. They are diving, jumping, laughing, shouting, singing, rejoicing and interacting with one another. They are full to overflowing.

When they turn to go out of the river, the light of the water (Spirit) goes with them. Like tendrils of light following behind and around them. So the river is a light and where the people go, there are fingers of light everywhere piercing and illuminating the darkness.

They go to where they are led, bringing others back to the river with them. When they get to the water's edge, their friend decides how deep they will go. Sometimes they edge their way in slowly, standing in the shallows for a while before going deeper. Some head for deep waters immediately. But it's not until they venture to the depths that they are filled with the light (Spirit of God) to go out themselves to bring someone else in.

As more people go deep into the water, more light goes out into the darkness.

We are not to stay in the river all the time. But we are to go out into the darkness and bring someone in. Then we can go back to bask in the water of God's presence, glory and fullness.

Reflections in
Psalms & Prose

Don't Give Up

Do you feel like you are under the enemy's attack,
are you pushed and shoved from every side?
Does the weight of all your troubles bring your spirit down,
It just seems like nothings gonna turn out right?

Don't give up, look up to Him. Don't give in just look within.
your God is dwelling there with you.
Hold on tight, no letting go, you don't walk this path alone.
Don't give up, Don't give in, just look to Him.
Don't give up, Don't give in, just look to Him.

As you journey down lifes' road, there are joys and there are sorrows,
Through everything He stays right by your side.
He has purposed in His heart plans fulfilled in your tomorrows,
So hold fast, stay the course, keep doing right.

So fight on through this battle that you're in,
Don't give up, make excuses or cave in,
For you know that God is with you, He will never leave your side.
He will guide and direct you, be your strength when you are tried.
Every weapon formed against you, He'll defend,

Don't give up, Don't give in, just look to Him.
Don't give up, Don't give in, just look to Him.

Live the Dream

There's a dream down deep inside of us, at the axis of our souls,
it's a longing welling up inside, getting stronger as it grows.
A dream that has a life of its own, given by God above,
a dream, a life, a passion, full of hope and faith and love.

Work the dream, live the dream through your visions deep inside.
Don't hold back, take a chance and your dreams will come alive.
Do what you were created for, don't hold back an ounce,
don't be content to idly wait, but do those things that count.
Work the dream, live the dream, hold firm and take your stand.
Pursue that dream with all your might,
till you hold it in your hand.

Welcome to the Family

Welcome to the family, there's always room for more.
Be ready to receive a love, like none you've known before.
We try to live uprightly, but sometimes make mistakes.
So if you're not quite perfect, you've come to the right place.

God's people are a varied bunch, we bear many shapes and size
Some like to dress rather casual, others wear a suit and tie
But deep beneath our surface, we all are much the same
We struggle with lifes ups and downs and trust in Jesus name.

We love to come together, to learn about our Lord
We worship and sing praises, and read His Holy Word
We laugh and cry together, our joys and sorrows share
Then break His bread together and show how much we care.

For Such A Time As This

For such a time as this we were created, for this defining moment we were formed,
this minute in eternity was designed with us in mind.
For such a time as this we were born.

Through the annuls of time God has called us, to a purpose far beyond what we can see, times to stand and be counted for the causes that are righteous,
times to sacrifice our own desires for a passionate endeavor,
to faithfully hold firm to God's design, to accomplish His plan for all mankind.

Many men and women down through history, came to that moment of decision in their lives, they stood fixed in their conviction not turning right of left,
they pursued the course of freedom putting God's truth to the test,
they discovered the plan within their plight,
as they stood strong and courageous in their fight.

Let us hold firm in our resolve to lift our banners high, to accomplish all that God has for our lives. To fully live each day reaching out to those around,
with love, honor and compassion in humanity's fight.

For such a time as this YOU were created, for this defining moment you were formed, this minute in eternity was designed with You in mind.
For such a time as this you were born.

Passionate Pursuit

Chasing after you, my love, only to be caught, caught up in the wonder of Your love.
Seeking after You, Beloved, only to be found, found in the embrace of God above.

It's the dance that we do, chasing only to be caught, pursuing the one of our dreams. Arms outstretched as we seek, looking only to be found,
engaging the creator of all things.

Chasing after you, my Love, only to be caught,
loving you with heart and soul and mind.
Seeking after you, Beloved, only to be found, basking in Your presence is my delight.

It's the motion of our lives, bowing down then lifted up, held in the arms of our King. It's the freedom that we find when we're captured by His love,
all things obtained when we surrender everything.

Such a passionate pursuit, first You and finally me,
realizing the depth of Your love.
What a wondrous way to live, pursued by love divine,
turning round to find myself held in Your arms.

Held By Your Love

As my eyes flutter open in the morning.
I smile gently cause you wait for me to come.
I rise quietly, moving to our special place,
Now I'm held by Your love, I'm compelled by Your love,
Like a magnet I am drawn to You Lord.

How can this be, that the God of all creation
Should desire to have me close to His heart?
As I feel Your loving presence now surround me
I am held by Your love, I'm compelled by Your love,
Like a magnet I am drawn to You Lord.

Who am I that you should take the time to notice,
That you would gaze at my entrance with such joy.
Just one look into your eyes was all I needed,
Now I'm held by Your love, I'm compelled by Your love,
Like a magnet I am drawn to You Lord.

It's true, but amazing that the High Lord of Heaven
waits expectantly for me to do my part.
Captivated with the thought that You adore me
I am held by Your love, I'm compelled by Your love,
Like a magnet, I am drawn to You Lord.

I Have Found a Man

I am a woman, a Samaritan, who has lived so foolishly,
I have yearned for love and value all my life.
He is a Jew, a man of honor, offering me 'A living water',
looking deep inside my soul with such insight.

What a wonderful thought, that this man of righteousness
can look at me with tenderness and care.
Surely He does not know all the things that I have done,
yet His words tell me, yes, that He's aware.

At last, I have found a man, a man that truly knows me,
someone who can see through all my lies.
He is here, I have found Him, a man so far above me,
yet I see love and compassion in His eyes,
so much love and compassion in His eyes.

This is the man I've dreamed of and searched for all my days
the one who offers me a brand new life.
This is the Christ, the Messiah, the one who knows me best,
and still I see the love that's in His eyes,
there is value and acceptance in His eyes.

Come see this man who knows me best, who quenched my deepest
thirst.
He offers life and peace within, deliverance from your curse.
Come hear His words of wisdom, look deep into His eyes,
You'll find true adoration and new purpose for your life.

Prepare Me

(the song from my dream of heaven in Anderson Alaska in 1993)

Prepare me, prepare me, prepare me to walk with Thee.
Prepare me, prepare me, prepare me to walk with Thee.

Lord I quiet myself and I seek You. I listen for the echo of Your voice.
I yield to the leading of Your precious Holy Spirit.
I follow You gladly, that's my choice.

Lord, I know Your ways are perfect. I long to surrender to Your will.
Please lead me in the plan You have designed just for me.
And with Your Holy Spirit I am filled.

I run down roads You've set before me. I dance before You, oh my King.
I give songs of praise, to You my voice I raise,
as You teach and instruct me, I will sing.

Prepare me, prepare me, prepare me to walk with Thee.
Prepare me, prepare me, prepare me to walk with Thee.

Honored to Bow

I am honored to bow at Your feet, Oh Lord.
I am honored to bow at Your feet, right here.
To kneel down and worship, to love You my King.
I am honored to bow down, I am honored to worship,
I am honored to love You, my Lord.

Once there was a woman, rejected and despised.
No one took notice, no one looked her in the eyes.
Then she met the Savior, who loved her and forgave,
He drew her out of her darkness, her life and soul to save.

The woman came to Jesus and bowed down at His feet.
She humbly knelt before Him, showing love as she did weep.
She washed His feet so gently with her tears and long dark hair.
And she showed her adoration for her Savior sitting there.

Let us all be humbled, Let us all bow low.
Let us put aside our pride, our praise and love now show.

I am honored to bow at Your feet, Oh Lord.
I am honored to bow at Your feet, right here.
To kneel down and worship, to love You my King.
I am honored to bow down, I am honored to worship,
I am honored to love You, my Lord.

Only Touch Him

I am sick and so lonely, I am struggling to breathe,
I'm weakened and so weary falling to my knees.
I'm pressing ever forward, how thick can this crowd be,
I must get next to Jesus, He has power, I believe.

Hearing people talking as I push on through the throng,
He is on a mission so I follow right along.
Dare I interrupt Him, should I slow Him down?
He goes to heal a young girl who lives in the next town.

My steps begin to falter, I'm weak from bleeding out.
I cannot go much further, I'm filled with fears and doubt.
If I can only touch Him, I know that is the key.
For if I can only touch Him, then He'll be touching me.

The crowds press in around Him to hear His every word.
They know He holds the answers, His wisdom they have heard.
I mustn't let them stop me, this is my final plea.
I've given all my money to find a remedy.

I stretch my hand out toward Him, Oh God give me the strength,
Just a few more footsteps, walks the answer to my dreams.
The space begins to shorten, He's almost within reach.
For if I can only touch Him, then He'll be touching me.

Then suddenly it happens, the contact has been made.
I feel power coming from Him, flowing through my veins.
He knows that I have taken without asking first.
He looks around to find the one delivered from her curse.

I come before Him trembling, I can't hold back the tears.
I share with Him my story, my journey and my fears.
I humbly bow before Him, falling to my knees.
He says my faith has made me whole, my healing is complete.

Strength is coursing through me, my life has been redeemed.

I must go tell my family of the One who just touched me.
His touch will never leave me or the love that's in His eyes.
That moment stands suspended as healing flowed from His body
into mine.

His touch is what I longed for, His touch is all I need.
To be here close beside Him, to know that He loves me.
I knew if I could touch Him, I knew that was the key.
For if I could only touch Him, then HE would be touching me.

There is now a spring to my step as I turn to go my way.
For a moment I gaze after Him as a child He goes to save.
There is such peace and comfort, I feel so light and free,
since I reached out to touch Him, and NOW HE is touching me.

Favor of God

The favor of God is mine, I have what He says I can.
Through Him, I can do all things, upon His Word I now stand. The
favor of God is for me, He looks on me with great love.
His will for my life is the very best, blessings rain down from Heaven
above.

The favor of God, the favor of God, His face is turned toward me.
The favor of God, the favor of God, He has blessings to pour over me.
The favor of God, the favor of God, His promises are true.
The favor of God, the favor of God, He provides everything for me
and you.

In the favor of God I rest secure, even when the dark days arrive.
He guides me through with His right hand and gives power to
overcome for my life.

Favor, He gives us favor. The favor of God is for You and me.
Favor, He gives us favor. The favor of God is for You and me.

I am the head and not the tail, I'm from above not beneath.
His face shines down upon me, coming or going, awake or asleep.

Fully Engaged

Fully engaged in Your plan Lord, urgently pursuing Your way.
Seeking the place where You need me, pushing in close day by day.

Fully engaged, pressing onward, ready to go, secure to move.
Fully engaged, I'm going forward, fully engaged, Your plan is true.

Fully engaged, who you've created, ready to fill Your plan and call.
Touching the lives of those around me, showing Your love and grace
to all.

Fully engaged, centered in Your will, stepping through doors You've
led me to,
choosing to follow Your best way, pursuing Your will, pursuing You.

Fully engaged, I'm going Your way. Seeking Your face, I'll follow
through.
You set the course, showed us the path, Lord. Not looking back, I'm
focused on You.

No Other Way

'No other way', the words echoed loud and long.
'No other way', up and down the heavenly halls.
'No other way', the Father decreed that day. 'It must be done, no other way.'

Would anyone be willing to do so much and who could do such a ponderous thing?
All heaven paused and wondered in awe
as from the throne room stepped their king.

'No other way', the Spirit whispered through His tears.
'No other way', He spoke out clear and pure.
'No other way', the Spirit decreed that day. 'It must be done, No other way'.

Waiting, the Father gazed upon His Son, as He said 'I Will' in a gentle voice.
'It isn't fair' the angels cried aloud. 'No one makes me do this.
It's my choice. It's my choice!'

'No other way', Jesus spoke out firm and strong.
'No other way', His voice rang sure and true.
'No other way', the Son decreed that day. 'It must be done, No Other Way'.

The sin of mankind demanded a price. The payment was death upon a cross.
The Son removed His heavenly robes and became a man compelled by love.

'No other way' the angels sang out as He turned.
'No other way', they bowed before their King.
'No other way', they lined His path to Heaven's gates.
'It must be done, it must be done, it must be done. There is no other way!'

Come, My Child

Come, Come, Come my child, Seek me while you may,
Don't hold back any of your heart, come to me today.

Come my child draw near to me, let me dry your tears.
Come, Believe and trust in me, let me erase all your fears.

Come my child, I love you so, I want to hold you near.
You are mine, I delight in you, come to me, I'm here.

Come my child, I paid the price to wash away your sin.
Come to me, I wait for you to invite me in again.

I gave my life, I gave it all, I'm here right now, please heed my call.

Come, Come, Come my child, Seek me while you may,
Don't hold back any of your heart, come to me today.

Holy, Just and Pure

I come to You as Savior, I bow to You, my King.
I sing to You, my Beloved, I talk with You, my Friend.
I hide in You, my Fortress, I fight within Your strength.
I follow You, my Shepherd, I rest deep in Your peace.

Savior, Redeemer, merciful and true, Almighty and Unchanging.
You are holy, just and pure.

I call upon my Healer, I stand strong in Your might.
You are my True and Faithful One. You are my Guiding Light.
I love You, my sweet Savior. I dance before You, Lord.
I sing to You this song of praise, today and forevermore.

Consume Me With All Of You

Consume me with all of You, Oh Lord I want to see Your face.
Consume me with all of You, I love to dwell within Your grace.
Your awesome love overwhelms my heart, Lord You lift me up and
refresh my life.

With all my heart, with all my soul, with all my mind and strength,
I look to You, I cling to You, Oh loving Savior.
With all I feel, with all I am, my thoughts are stayed on You.
I need you near, I want You here, my loving Savior.

Consume me, with all of You, till You I cannot contain.
Consume me with all of You, Your presence flow through me again.
Your wondrous peace, floods over all of me.
I drink in all of You, till Your precious face I see.

Consume me, melt me, mold me, make me. Consume me, fill me
with all of You.

Consume me with all of You, Almighty King to You I bow.
Consume me, with all of You, Oh Lord please fill me with You now.

I Love You, Lord

ant You, Lord. I need You, Lord, I do.
ant You, Lord. I need You, Lord, I do.

In our quiet times together, you whisper in my ear,
words of peace and understanding and of love.
I love our moments together, when I feel You surround me,
with the comfort of Your presence, like a dove.

In my time of pain and sorrow, and in my time of grief,
You are the One I call on, and You come.
When life is more than heavy and my face is streaked with tears,
You are the friend who holds me, till I'm done.

Because of Your presence, I can face the trials of life
and be a living witness of Your love.
I'll shine Your light around me, I'll share Your peace and joy
with those You put in my path, I will love.

I love You, Lord. I want You, Lord. I need You, Lord, I do.
I love You, Lord. I want You, Lord. I need You, Lord, I do.

I Am Loved

I wanted to be in His presence, I needed to be close to Him. But I am so imperfect, I long to be holy and cleansed. I hesitantly entered His domain, wondering if I could draw near. He had said I could come anytime, to speak His name and He would hear.

So forward I walked to His throne, from a distance I saw Him sitting there. He was laughing and talking with the Father, golden waves and rainbows everywhere. Then He turned and as our eyes met, His face beamed forth with joy. A welcoming gleam of adoration, pierced right through to my soul.

I am loved, I am accepted. I am loved, I am adored. I am loved, I'll never doubt it.
I am loved, I am loved, I am loved.

Come on in, He sits there waiting. Come to Him, He looks for You. Do not fear, His love is reaching. He's provided a way to make it through. His arms are spread out to receive you, it matters not what you have done. His eyes are filled with adoration, He offers you forgiveness and love.

You are loved, you are accepted. You are loved, you are adored. You are loved, don't ever doubt it. You are loved, you are loved, you are loved.

I Worship You, Almighty God

Your name is high, above all names, I bow down low before You, Lord.
Your love is deep, much deeper than the sea, I stand in awe before Your throne.
Always near, ready to hear, my faintest cry, my deepest woe.
Lifting me up, filling my cup, your arms hold me close in Your love.

I worship You, I worship You, I worship You, Almighty God.

You are my Lord, You are my dearest friend, my life is sustained in Your hand.
You're always there, You hear my every prayer, with You in victory, I shall stand.
Walking with You, talking with You, I long to enter in to Your embrace.
Sharing our love, grace from above, You hold me close all of my days.

I worship You, I worship You, I worship You, Almighty God.

Holy are You Lord

Great are You Lord and I praise You forevermore.
Awesome are You Lord and I bow down to You.
Wonderful and Marvelous, Righteous and True,
Holy are You Lord and I worship You.

Mighty are You Lord and I stand in Your strength.
Gracious are You Lord and I abide secure in You.
Adoring and Merciful, Compassionate and Just,
Holy are You Lord and I worship You.

I worship You, I worship You, I bow before my King.
I worship You, I worship You, This offering of praise I bring
Holy, Holy, Holy is the Lord. Worthy, worthy, worthy is the Lord.

Gentle are You Lord and I seek Your loving face.
Glorious are You Lord and I yearn to be with You.
Patient and Faithful, Forgiving and Kind,
Holy are You Lord and I worship You.

In The Glory of Your Presence

Lord, I push aside the trials of life. I turn away from my busy day.
I step back from my worries and fears, I enter in and to You draw
near.

Like stepping through a veil of mist, like pressing through a
waterfall I'm kissed.
I'm drenched in the very essence of You, when I enter the glory of
Your presence.

Lord I choose to come, I choose to seek for the glory of Your presence.
It is my desire to know You more and to be in the glory of Your
presence.

Like standing tall on a mountains height, the warmth of You wraps
around me tight.
Like gentle snow on my upturned face, Your peace and love rest
upon me.

Like the bubbling laughter of a happy child, as she swings up high
toward the sky,
You fill me with such a wondrous joy as I dwell in the glory of Your
presence.

In Your Embrace

Oh Lord I praise You, Oh Lord I come, to now make mention of Your great love.
How vast, how endless, it flows to me in waves of glory, eternally.
Oh loving Savior, in Your embrace, I dwell in safety, I rest in grace,
You hold me gently in loving arms of tender mercy, throughout life's storms.

How can I fathom, your depth of love, it washes o'er me from springs above.
How vast, how timeless, how pure and sweet, Your love engulfs me and calls me deep.
I dare not leave You, I must not stray, I need You near me both night and day.
I dance before You, I sing Your praise, Oh loving Savior, in Your embrace.

In Your embrace Lord, I find sweet peace, the cares of life Lord, I can release,
to see Your love shine as our eyes meet, as I draw closer in Your embrace.

Sweet Peace

A warm spring day, a gentle blowing breeze,
Windchimes softly playing melodies.
Birds of every color fluttering playfully,
The fragrance of roses bring sweet peace.

Fruit trees that are budding, the smell of fresh mown grass,
An ice cold glass of lemonade, so sweet.
Sitting in my rocker on such a lovely day,
Exudes and provides me with sweet peace.

But more than all these blessings, the fact that You are near
makes my heart to sing so joyfully,
My Lord and my Savior dwelling here with me
Fills me to overflowing with sweet peace.

Anointed to Love

There is an anointing not heard about much,
for it requires caring and giving and such.
It lays aside quarrels and prejudice alike.
It stretches out hands and not arms of might.

This anointing breaks walls with a kind word.
It penetrates barriers with a smile, not a sword.
Christ had this anointing, He shares it with us,
if we are but open, but receive it we must.

For people are hurting, His love's what they need.
We have been chosen to be His hands and feet.
Help us reach out to touch them as You do,
anointing of love please flow through us too

Hush-A-Bye (Tony's song)

Hush-a-bye, my little child, close your eyes and sleep.
Mama's here, to hold you near, so stretch and yawn and sleep.

Hush-a-bye, my little child, I press you to my cheek,
your funny smile makes me laugh a while, my love for you is deep.

Your heavenly angel hovers near, guarding your life you see,
God has a plan for you, little one, You are special and unique.

Hush-a-bye, my little child, I kiss your hands and feet,
my precious treasure from above, close your eyes and sleep,
my love for you is deep, so stretch and yawn and sleep.

Sleepy-Bye (Waylon's song)

It's time to go to sleepy-bye, your eyelids gently lower, Your little mouth,
it sweetly yawns as you nestle on my shoulder, as you nestle on my shoulder.

There are hugs and kisses plenty from family all around, so settle down my precious little one and go to sleepy-bye town, and go to sleepy-bye town.

It's time to go to sleepy-bye, no need to fuss or stew, so quieten down my little one, God watches over you, God watches over you.

How precious you are to me as we say your nightly prayers. Oh Lord please watch this little one, guarding angels everywhere.

It's time to go to sleepy-bye, the night is here so dream. Tomorrow holds adventures new, so close your eyes my sweet, so close your eyes my sweet.

Little Princess (Lacy's song)

When I look into your eyes I see beauty.
All the wonders of a precious little girl.
There are giggles, there are tickles, so much laughter,
As we spin and dance together in a whirl.

What a joy to see your brother giving kisses
Hear you chuckle when he blows upon your back.
See you smiling when your daddy hugs you gently,
Hear you sigh when mommy nuzzles on your neck

Chorus:
Close your eyes and sleep my little princess.
Rest peacefully and know that you are safe.
God and I will always keep a vigil
To protect and keep you every day.

I'm amazed at how God's blessed me with you darlin',
Just to think that He entrusts me with your care.
What a special gift you are from Him, my precious,
such an overwhelming love for you we share.

As I hold you in my arms and rock you gently,
speak soft words of love and caring in your ear.
As I watch your little eyelids droop in slumber,
Holy Angels gather round to hold you near.

Little Green Tractor
(Jordan's song)

It had been a long day, filled with school and play,
He had done all his work, it was the end of the day,
Played a while with the dog, watched a race on TV,
Went and grabbed a snack and then tried tickling me.

Found a game on the computer and played it a while,
He let a small yawn escape, then he said with a smile,
I guess I'll take me a bath and get ready for bed,
My favorite dream's awaiting, dancing round in my head.

Hey mom, I'll take you for a ride on my little green tractor,
You'll wanna go slow, but I'll make it go faster,
Off down the road and into the pasture,
It'll be alright, cause in my dreams it don't matter
I'll even let you drive, mom, that is, if you want to,
But in this dream we can fly like the birds do,
So just hold on tight, close your eyes if you'd rather,
We'll fly through the sky on my little green tractor.

So I gave him a hug and said get ready for bed,
Be sure you come and get me, 'fore you lay down that head.
This is one special dream, you're treating me to,
And I don't want to miss one minute with you.

Hey son, make room on that seat, Oh, here we go just you and me.

We'll rev up the engine and shine up the chrome,
We'll sail through God's heaven, then come on home,
Give thanks to the Lord, when we say your prayers,
Then take another trip with my son through the air.

Hey mom, I'll take you for a ride on my little green tractor,
You'll wanna go slow, but I'll make it go faster,
Off down the road and into the pasture,

Vonnie Behrend

It'll be alright, cause in my dreams it don't matter
I'll even let you drive, mom, that is, if you want to,
But in this dream we can fly like the birds do,
So just hold on tight, close your eyes if you'd rather,
We'll fly through the sky on my little green tractor.

At Last He Sleeps
(Wyatt's song)

Running everywhere, all around all around, darting here and there,
don't slow down, can't slow down.
Jumping, skipping, a twirling top, bouncing, laughing, dare not
stop,
if he slows to a steady pace, the sleepy yawns will fill his face.

So Climbing everywhere, up then down, what a clown, crawling
here and there,
won't slow down, can't slow down.
Leaping, hopping, flying high, whirling, soaring, full of life,
bedtime's here, he's almost done, his steps slow down, here comes
that yawn.

Mommy's arms look so inviting, Daddy's snuggles finding him.
Prayers and words are softly spoken, big blue eyes begin to dim.
Slowly, gently sleep is coming, a lullaby to him they sing,
drifting where the dreams are waiting, carried there on angel's
wings

Sleep little one, the games will wait, tomorrow's adventures will
keep.
Sleep little one, the tickles will be there when in the morning we
meet.
Mommy, Daddy know the struggle, holding him in loving arms,
wiggles now give way to slumber, tucking blankets snug and warm.

Still he fights the sleep that's coming, softly crying in gentle arms,
hugs and kisses ease his tussle, finally dreams possess his calm.
Sighing, smiling, off he travels, to a land of ponies and sheep,
stretching, yawning his surrender, thank You Lord, at last he sleeps.

Sweet, Precious Child
(Tayla's song)

Sweet, precious child, we love you, You bring such a joy to our life.
Sharing sweet imagination, With family and playthings alike.
Here you come racing and springing, Full of life, like a whirling top spins
Climbing and leaping and laughing, Twinkling eyes and mischievous grin.

Your heart is so tender and loving, Young and old you count as a friend
Reaching out to comfort the hurting, Here you come to the rescue again.
Playing dolls and then some dress up, These girl games can be kind of fun
More exciting is tending the critters, And helping daddy clean his gun.

Little sister, who loves her brother, helping Mommy to tend to his needs
Speaking gentle words to calm him, when his crying will not cease.
God sees your heart so caring, and is pleased with all of your ways.
So keep on following Jesus and find happiness throughout your days.

Sweet, precious child, we love you, You bring such a joy to our life.
Sharing sweet imagination, With family and playthings alike.

Rock-A-Bye (Travis' song)

Rock a bye my little one, the sun has set, the day is done.
Hush a bye, I'll dry your tears, your loving family gathers near.
As I hold you close to me, close those sparkling eyes in sleep.
Snuggle close within my arms, you are safe from every harm.
Rock a bye my little one, go to sleep and dreams will come
Hush a bye, now settle down, rest as angels gather round

As I tickle fluffy cheeks, trusting eyes gaze up at me,
Tiny fingers grab the air, cooing giggles everywhere.
Roly poly legs kick high, chubby arms bat at the sky
As I nuzzle peach fuzz hair, your baby scent floats through the air.

Rock a bye my little one, the sun has set, the day is done.
Hush a bye, I'll dry your tears, loving family always near.
As I rock you here tonight, Squeeze my finger oh so tight
Close your eyes and drift away to wake up in a brand new day.
Rock a bye my little one, go to sleep and dreams will come
Hush a bye, now settle down, rest as angels gather round.

Rain Down From Heaven

Pour over me, sweet Holy Spirit.
Saturate me with Your presence.
Rain down from heaven, the very nearness of You,
Come now and drench me, in the essence of You.

I stand here waiting, expecting and longing,
hands lifted upward, looking only for You.
Rain down from heaven, the very presence of You,
come now and soak me, in the sweetness of You.

You are the One that I long for,
You are the air that I breathe,
Life does not hold any flavor,
when I don't sense that You're near.

My pulse starts to quicken, at the sound of Your coming,
my breathing grows shallow, awaiting Your touch.
Rain down from heaven, the very beauty of You,
Come now embrace me, with the fragrance of You.

You're like the sunshine that warms me,
You speak, I feel the evening breeze,
the sense of Your closeness enthralls me,
the warmth of Your embrace surrounds me.

My Brother's Keeper

Am I my brother's keeper? The question has been asked,
from the very beginning of time and shall be to the last.
Am I my brother's keeper? So many people say,
"Am I required to look out for him and assist along the way?"

Should I step in at the school yard when a bully's pushing low,
the little lanky shy guy whose muscles have yet to grow?
Should I intrude when a woman, is screaming in the alley,
and gather neighbors with me, so around her we can rally?
Should I aid a little lost girl who is crying for her dad,
should I help her find her way back home, forgoing some of my plans?

Am I my brother's keeper, should I care if He lives or dies,
when he follows a cruel dictator and listens to his lies?
Am I my brother's keeper, when he's lying almost dead,
bruised and beaten by the roadside or do I turn my head?

The Word of God is very clear, and we must heed its call.
We ARE our brother's keeper, and we must give our all.
Sometimes he's been so beaten, lied to and deceived,
we have to reach a helping hand and meet him at his need.
I am my brother's keeper, the message seems so clear.
We are required to love and help each other far and near.

An Intimate God

There is a God who loves you,
There is a God Who wants to hold you near.
There is a God who hears you.
There is a God who speaks your name with tenderness and care.

He wants you to come to Him-----------------He will wait
He wants you to follow Him-------------------He will linger
He wants you to pursue Him--------------------He will slow down
He wants you to seek after Him---------------He will be found.

He wants to draw you into His arms.
He wants to wipe away your tears.
He wants to make you laugh with joy.
He wants to dance with you with singing.

Come right now and call Him friend.
Come right now and call Him Savior.
Come right now and call Him Lord.
Come right now and call Him, my Love.

He is here, waiting just for you.
Don't question any longer.
This is real, not a fantasy.
The God of the Universe, the Creator of everything
IS concerned with you, you are significant to Him.
He created you are for a reason.
Your talents, gifts, quirks and personality were made just for you,
so that you can fill that special place in eternity,
that needs someone just like you.
You are fearfully and wonderfully made.
And God loves You!!